Contemporary
sociology of
the school
*General editor*
JOHN EGGLESTON

# The sociology of
educational innovation

# CONTEMPORARY SOCIOLOGY
## OF THE SCHOOL

PAUL BELLABY
The sociology of comprehensive schooling

BRIAN DAVIES
Social control and education

SARA DELAMONT
Interaction in the classroom

JOHN EGGLESTON
The ecology of the school

ERIC HOYLE
School organization and administration

COLIN LACEY
The socialization of teachers

PETER MUSGRAVE
The moral curriculum: a sociological analysis

PHILIP ROBINSON
Education and poverty

MICHAEL STUBBS
Language, schools and classrooms

WILLIAM TYLER
The sociology of educational inequality

TOM WHITESIDE
The sociology of educational innovation

TOM WHITESIDE

# The sociology of educational innovation

METHUEN

First published in 1978 by Methuen & Co Ltd
11 New Fetter Lane, London EC4P 4EE
© 1978 Tom Whiteside
Printed in Great Britain
by Richard Clay (The Chaucer Press) Ltd,
Bungay, Suffolk

ISBN (hardback) 0 416 55820 8
ISBN (paperback) 0 416 55830 5

# CONTENTS

Editor's introduction 7

1 Innovation – the name of the game 11

2 The counter-attack on innovation 22

3 The extent and the nature of the change 32

4 The prospect of planned social change 44

5 Case studies of change 59

6 Innovation and the community 80

7 Students and innovation 97

8 Conclusion 106

References and name index 113

Subject index 123

# Editor's introduction

Sociology has changed dramatically in the past decade. Sociologists have provided an ever increasing diversity of empirical and theoretical approaches that are advancing our understanding of the complexities of societies and their educational arrangements. It is now possible to see the over-simplification of the earlier sociological view of the world running smoothly with agreed norms of behaviour, with institutions and individuals performing functions that maintained society and where even conflict was restricted to 'agreed' areas. This normative view of society with its functionalist and conflict theories has now been augmented by a range of interpretative approaches in which the realities of human interaction have been explored by phenomenologists, ethnomethodologists and other reflective theorists. Together they have emphasized the part that individual perceptions play in determining social reality and have challenged many of the characteristics of society that the earlier sociologists had assumed to be 'given'.

The new approaches have had striking effects upon the sociology of the school. Earlier work was characterized by a range of incompletely examined assumptions about such matters as ability, opportunity and social class. Sociologists asked how working class children could achieve in the schools like middle class children. Now they also ask how a social system defines class, opportunities and achievement. Such concepts and many others such as subjects, the curriculum and even schools themselves are seen to be products of the social system in which they exist. In our study of the school we can now explore more fully the ways in which individual teachers' and students' definitions of their situation help to determine its social arrangements; how perceptions of achievement can not only define achievement but also identify those who achieve; how expectations about schooling can determine the very nature and evaluation of schools.

This series of volumes explores the main areas of the sociology of the school in which new understanding of events is now available. Each introduces the reader to the new interpretations, juxtaposes them against the longer standing perspectives and reappraises the contemporary practice of education and its consequences.

In each, specialist authors develop their own analyses of central issues such as poverty, opportunity, comprehensive schooling, the language and interaction of the classroom, the teacher's role, the ecology of education, and ways in which education acts as an instrument of social control. The broad spectrum of themes and treatments is closely interrelated; it is offered to all who seek new illumination on the practice of education and to those who wish to know how contemporary sociological theory can be applied to educational issues.

For many observers, the most striking feature of contemporary schooling is innovation. Change seems to be continuous with new curricula, new forms of organization and new teaching methods taking place inside new styles of building with new kinds of equipment. Tom Whiteside uses a distinctively sociological analysis to probe the reality of this change. In what way is the experience of children and teachers different from that of the recent past? What are the politics of educational innovation – how are they played and what are their consequences? How does educational innovation illuminate the exercise of power in the school system and does it reveal any changes in the use and distribution of that power?

The study of educational innovation is central to most of the contemporary debates about the changing nature of schooling, yet, until the publication of this book, the evidence has been fragmentary; the argument spasmodic. In his wide-ranging and comprehensive analysis Tom Whiteside has brought our knowledge together coherently and in doing so has valuably augmented it. His book is likely to be of major importance to all who seek to understand the realities of change in the contemporary school.

John Eggleston

# 1

# Innovation – the name of the game

The unprecedented post-war expansion in formal education at all levels has been called 'the schooling explosion'. In advanced industrial countries, capitalist, socialist and communist, governments have committed themselves to universal primary and secondary schooling, a lengthening of compulsory schooling and to an enlargement of the age group who go on to higher education. While some commentators have tended to over-emphasize the 'egalitarian revolution' produced by this explosion, particularly in relation to changes in secondary and higher education, most countries have proudly boasted of reductions in illiteracy, increasing shares of the Gross National Product devoted to education, and an ever-increasing proportion of the population enrolled in primary, secondary and higher education. For example, in Britain, public expenditure as a whole rose by 82·9 per cent between 1953 and 1972 (at constant 1970 prices) while public expenditure on education rose by 242·9 per cent (Klein *et al.*, 1974). Economists have pointed out that, apart from electronics and natural gas, higher education grew faster than any major national enterprise in the 1960s (Layard *et al.*, 1969, p. 1).

There were strong demographic pressures for expansion in this period. The 1972 Education White Paper stated 'In the 1960s the main determinant of rising educational expenditure was the increasing number of young people using the educational system. The expansion was led by quantitative, or demographic factors; larger age groups within the span of compulsory education; rising demand for access to sixth forms and more staff to teach them' (Department of Education and Science, 1972, p. 1). Alongside this demographic pressure for expansion there was an increase in the social demand for education. As education became, and was seen to become, the avenue for better jobs, so the demand for educational qualifications grew, setting up an inflationary spiral in which the value of any given level of education was deflated by rising qualification requirements for jobs. This increased demand for education was in part due to the changed economic situation. In the immediate post-war years the economic and social dislocation made this largely a period of reconstruction. The 'full employment' and economic growth of the 1950s contributed to generally higher standards of living in what became labelled by the end of the decade 'The Affluent Society'.

The apparently secure technological foundations provided by capitalism and the promise of future mass abundance made it possible to think of a new order of society that would end 'the dark ages of poverty and want and [take] mankind forward to a future which our fathers could not have dreamed possible' (Wilson, 1964, p. 3). This view of a new social order incorporated a redefinition of the role of schooling and among some Labour Party politicians education came to be viewed as a serious alternative to nationalization in promoting a more just and efficient society (Halsey, 1968). The intellectual foundation for political programmes which emphasized education's central role in producing social equality was, in part, laid down in the writings of social scientists who proclaimed a changed role for education in advanced industrial societies. Floud and Halsey, in their introduction to the influential reader, *Education, Economy and Society*, saw the educational system as occupying a new and 'strategic place as a central determinant of the economic, political, social and cultural character of a society' (Halsey *et al.*, 1961, p. 3). Educational inequalities were seen as particularly important because they became, in effect, fundamentally determinant of all social inequality.

At the same time economists were particularly popular in that they appeared to offer 'objective' assessments, indicating that at the societal level further investments in education were a favourable alternative to other uses of resources and that at the individual level investments in schooling yielded ample returns in the form of higher life-time earnings. Thus, increasing expenditure on education could be defended because education was an investment, an investment whose yield could be calculated. The prominence of economic arguments can be seen from the educational reports of the period. The 1956 White Paper on Technical Education argued that other countries were making determined efforts to train more scientific and technical manpower, and that Britain, too, must do the same, the aims being 'to strengthen the foundations of our economy, to improve the living standards of our people' (Ministry of Education, 1956, p. 4). The Robbins Report on Higher Education (1963) stated that of the four objectives essential to a properly balanced system of higher education the first was 'instruction in skills suitable to play a part in the general division of labour'. On the other side of the Atlantic there was a corresponding belief – President Kennedy, in submitting a National Education Improvement Act of 1963 to Congress, said 'This nation is committed to economic growth, and recent research has shown that one of the most beneficial of all such investments is education, accounting for some 40 per cent of the nation's growth and productivity in recent years. In the new age of science and space, improved education is essential to give meaning to our initial purpose and power' (Harbison and Myers, 1964, p. 159). Thus the expansion of education which was conceived of as a necessary democratic precondition of faster economic growth could also be justified in terms of its more direct economic yield. The economic and social goals connected with education were seen as mutually supportive; more education supposedly meant both more well-trained people and greater opportunity for the under-privileged.

However, at this time the interest of social scientists was mainly in the structure of education and its relationships with wider societal structures rather than in the internal relationships, curriculum, teaching methods and personal styles of behaviour that constituted the greater part of educational study (Vaizey and

Clarke, 1976). The foreword to *Education, Economy and Society* saw sociology making a contribution to the understanding of education in modern society by analysing important aspects of the wider social structure in which policy-makers, administrators and teachers were working. This level of approach particularly appealed as the results of public opinion polls in the 1950s convinced Labour Party politicians that the way to gain acceptance for comprehensive schools probably lay in stressing, not the egalitarian virtues of the schools, but rather the opportunities they offered to all children of getting a 'grammar school education'. Though it was recognized that change, particularly in the bodies of knowledge and belief transmitted within the educational system, would be necessary, this was seen as outside the province of the sociologist and something best left to the educationist. The consequent stress on 'efficiency' in the provision of educational opportunities was later sharply criticized for its lack of interest in the educational system and the failure to consider what political definitions of equality might mean in terms of the everyday workings of schools, particularly comprehensive schools (see, for example, Marsden, 1972).

The feeling among many educationists at this time was that the new relationship between education and the rest of society would require major changes in the style as well as the content of education. There was a resurgence of the belief that educational institutions were failing to respond to economic and social changes within the wider society. So pervasive was the theme of innovation that some felt it essential to point out that innovation was not of necessity a good thing and hardened veterans in staffrooms across the country were suggesting that those who wished to promote their careers and make a name for themselves would be wise to be innovative even if the innovative process proved to be undesirable. As Goodlad observed, during the 1960s innovation was the name of the education game (Goodlad *et al.*, 1974). During this period an increasingly complex apparatus, both national and international, was built up to create and disseminate new approaches to schooling.

Though there was a high level of consensus among educational opinion-makers on the need for change, during this period there was, and still continues to be, a wide variation in the scope of the

14

changes envisaged. The alternatives proposed ranged all the way from leaving the present school virtually intact as an institution but with much revision in curriculum and instruction to replacing completely the school with new arrangements for education with or without some form of compulsory education. Following Hoyle (1972, p. 33), we can identify three broad approaches to educational innovation.

## 1  To modify the system

Much educational writing contains suggestions for producing modifications of the present system. In this country attempts to produce alterations while maintaining the main features of the system can be seen in the emergence of interest in curriculum development, conceived of mainly in terms of subject renewal. In a society felt to be dependent to an unprecedented extent on the results of scientific research, it is not surprising to find that science was the branch of knowledge where pressure for reform of syllabuses was strongest; the argument being that rapid developments in the knowledge areas of pure science and technology had made much of the existing curriculum clearly out of date. The Association for Science Education provided a channel for science teachers to express their dissatisfaction with syllabuses and was influential in persuading the Nuffield Foundation, a charitable trust, to initiate the first of a series of substantial curriculum development projects in December 1961. This emphasis on an updated subject-matter can be seen in the following extract describing thinking at the time of the setting up of the Schools Council, the major curriculum body in England and Wales.

In this, as in many other countries, there has been a growing consciousness of the need to reappraise syllabuses and curricula. Until comparatively recently changes in the school curriculum have taken place only through the slow spread of ideas among teachers (helped by the efforts of H.M. Inspectors) or through the work of committees set up for some specific purpose. The rate of change did not keep pace with the needs of the times or provide a speedy response to developments in particular branches of knowledge or to changes in the general

15

view about the aims of education. (Department of Education and Science, 1966, p. 1)

Alongside this concern for a revised subject-matter there grew a new emphasis on how children learn, the virtues of activity, discovery and inquiry methods with a stress on new ways of breaking down and organizing subject-matter. In this development one major influence was Bruner (1966) who linked the academic interest in updated curriculum content with the more pedagogical interest in teaching and learning, arguing that reform of curriculum content and changes in learning and teaching procedures must go hand in hand. In the main these changes could be accommodated with the existing framework of the school.

## 2  To transform the system

For some educationists changes solely in curriculum and teaching and learning styles were not radical enough. Many critics were concerned to bring about a more far-reaching transformation in the school system. Many who argued for radical change in the school system utilized the vocabulary associated with the vision of a new social order, relating their proposals for changes in school systems to changes that had occurred or were likely to occur in society. They argued from a functionalist standpoint that the rate of societal change was such that schools would not be able to resist the pressures for change generated and, therefore, change was inevitable. Thus Gass, as Director of the Centre for Educational Research and Innovation of OECD, writes in the preface to a series of case studies on educational innovation that 'it is not feasible to expect a standstill in the school while at the same time accepting a rapid process of economic, technological and cultural change in the wider community' (Gass, 1973, p. 3). The promoters thus attempt to justify large-scale changes in educational institutions in terms of bringing them into line with the rest of society, rather than in terms of educational institutions as active agents of change in the society.

The view of the future that was most prevalent was a similar one to that of Halsey *et al*, (1961), one that presumed that advanced industrial societies were moving from a production of goods economy based on physical labour to a distribution of services economy based on mental abilities. Bell (1974), for example, wrote of the growth of a new 'intelligentsia' – professionals working in the 'non-profit' sector including educators, medical health specialists, social scientists, mental health workers – and predicted a substantial increase in the non-profit human services during the 1970s and the 1980s. Frequently incorporated into such views were beliefs that non-manual jobs would replace manual jobs with a subsequent increase in worker satisfaction; that automation would reduce the number of unskilled and semi-skilled manual jobs to insignificance; and that we were entering an age of mass leisure. These beliefs have now been vigorously challenged. While there has been a decline in the proportion of unskilled jobs, it is realized that most jobs remain, and are likely to remain, dull and boring. The unvaried routine of work, the simplicity of most tasks and the constant supervision characteristic of hierarchical settings are likely to continue to deny to the majority of workers a sense of competence and a feeling of responsibility. The white-collar jobs are often routine, the 'leisure revolution' has not occurred and, where increased time has become available, many workers have 'moonlighted', i.e. sought second jobs (Grubb and Lazerson, 1975).

Recognition of some of these inconsistencies has led other innovators to develop within the same framework more sophisticated rationales for changing educational institutions. This is exemplified in a document sent to the parents of Countesthorpe College, an innovative upper secondary school in Leicestershire. This school was seen by its first Warden, McMullen, as attempting to minimize what he saw as the growing conflict in secondary schools between teachers and taught and between teachers and the head. Upon opening, the school was proudly thought of as different from other educational institutions and was thought, by some, to provide the model for the new type of comprehensive school. Its significant innovations fitted into a set of projected trends in secondary education – towards a freer curriculum, wider participation in the running of schools, the abandonment of old rituals and the move to new styles of teacher–pupil relationships. In a document, sent prior to the opening of the school, explaining its purposes and why it would be different from more traditional educational institutions, the Warden stressed the increasing rapidity of social change and the inappropriateness of a traditional education because of changes in the world between 1975 and 2025. This was the period during which the present generation of schoolchildren would live their adult lives.

The picture presented of the future society was a familiar one: immense changes in technology rendering particular skills out of date, increased job switching, increased geographical mobility and increased leisure time. The implications of this view of the future for schooling were clearly brought out:

> the individual who will achieve satisfaction over this coming half century must have a clear sense of his own identity and ability, must have developed intellectual and emotional strategies that make for adaptation to change. Emotional satisfaction must come entirely from his relationships with the small groups he lives, plays and works with, but these may change over his lifetime and may involve others from differing social and racial backgrounds. He is unlikely to develop an absolute ethos that will serve him for the fifty years of his adult life; he will need to decide on ethical guide lines at any given moment, but he must also be prepared to re-examine them in the light of changing social structures and organization in the face of shorter working hours and less exacting or stimulating work, he will have to develop a full life outside his working hours, one that allows him intellectual, emotional and physical actions that bring satisfaction (McMullen, 1968, p. 65).

This rationale appears still to be accepted by Watts, the new Warden of the College (Watts, 1973a; Watts, 1977, p. 28).

## 3 To abolish the system

During the late 1960s and the early 1970s another group of critics put forward a view of the schools which saw them not merely as reflections of society but as curbing thinking to the point of being anti-intellectual, condemning children to years of inhumane incarceration and failing to challenge or stimulate. The titles of their books, *Deschooling Society, Compulsory Miseducation, How Children Fail* and *Death at an Early Age*, proclaim the nature of their

18

criticism. The suggestions for remedying the assumed conditions range from schools in which children are set free to no schools at all. For Illich (1971) and Reimer (1971), for example, it is an undeniable human right that all those who want to learn should have access to available resources for learning at any time in their lives. This would be achieved by the provision of various 'networks', including direct access to resources for learning such as museums and libraries, the establishment of 'skill exchanges' and other devices which would bring together both learners and those who possess the skills they wish to acquire.

## Innovation and the expert

In this chapter, so far, we have explored the scope and extent of change envisaged by supporters of different types of educational innovation. Clearly implicit in such views are different conceptions of the relationship between education and society as well as different views of the degree of change required within the present society. Whereas those involved in the development of curriculum innovation have had only limited objectives in these areas, those attempting to transform the school system have more clearly developed and broader objectives in these areas. Education is seen as playing a key part in bringing about a new type of social order, reminiscent of Karl Mannheim's views on the role of education in reconstructing the social order along the lines of a 'Third Way' leading out of liberal-capitalist waste and inefficiency and away from the 'satanic efficiency of brutal dictators' (Remmling, 1975). Critics of Mannheim have pointed out how in his work there is an uneasy relationship between 'planning for democracy' and 'democratic planning' and the same tension appears in the writings of many of the proponents of radical change in education. As we have seen, they have frequently presented their accounts of innovation in terms either of the changes needed in schooling to bring it into line with a changing society or the changes needed to allow its students to cope with a future society. The non-evaluative technological tone of these accounts has meant that even questions about the ends of education are seen as removed from the sphere of politics, soluble by 'science' and hence the domain of the technical expert. For example, during the 1960s and 1970s, the

19

science of futurology has played an important part in legitimating the claims made by innovators. A futurologist is a person who, by extrapolating from present trends and identifying the likely consequences of policies before they have been translated into action, claims to be able to give a detailed picture of a possible future, or preferably of alternative futures which are dependent on decisions taken on critical issues. Reliance on such accounts has meant that the question of who plans the goals of education has been obscured by the promoters of innovation who have presented it as a value-neutral activity which was seen to be inevitable.

Such a view of innovation clearly de-emphasizes its social and political character – the fact that innovations are still means by which some people organize and control the lives of other people and their children according to their conceptions as to what is preferable. It disguises the reality that some people helped to plan the changes, that some people benefited from them while others did not, and that some consequences were intended while others were not. To take but one example, McMullen's picture of a future society was his vision. In its presentation there is a studied neglect of the problems of predicting societal futures and a seeming lack of awareness of alternative paths of development. Instead of such views of the future presenting critical choices for the members of the society, they are used to support the educationist's claim to determine the nature of educational ends. Some critics have charged that such utopian views of the future, ignoring as they do society's technical and instrumental needs, will in the long run be detrimental to bringing about change in society. Etzioni has reminded us that 'We must recognize that the transition from one societal pattern to another will not be abrupt, even if there will be a radical revolution, and a revolution does not seem imminent . . . Our efforts to prepare students for a society that may exist at a later date or for a society which cannot exist reduces the impact of the educational system as an agent of societal change' (Etzioni, 1971, p. 98).

In this book my main concern is not to study in detail specific curriculum innovations sponsored by outside bodies interested in getting such practices accepted into the general curricula of schools. Into such a category I would place, for example, Nuffield Science and Primary School French. Neither is it concerned with attempts at central or local government level to effect change by administrative re-organization. Rather it concentrates upon attempts made by individual primary and secondary schools to introduce into their schools educational practices loosely derived from 'progressive' educational theories. These attempts have involved a move to teaching and learning styles which de-emphasize the traditional directive, didactic role of the teacher and which stress the creative aspects of a student-centred approach. The integration of knowledge rather than its compartmentalization is an essential feature of this approach as is the shift of emphasis away from the assessment function of education.

Throughout the book it will be argued that decisions made about educational methods do not rest upon some kind of empirical evidence but are clearly rooted in political judgments and concepts of what constitutes a good person and a desirable society. Consideration will be given to the question of whose definitions of a good person and a desirable society are contained in progressive education. The problems arising from the difficulty these progressive policies have in gaining acceptance among some teachers, students, parents and the wider community who hold different educational conceptions will also be examined.

# 2

# The counter-attack on innovation

In the changed economic and demographic climate of the 1970s, where the expansion of education can no longer be regarded as inevitable, the vision of the 'new society' founded on schooling has come under attack from both the conservatives and the radicals. The intellectual underpinnings of the political programmes of the 1960s have been vigorously challenged by many social scientists forcing a reappraisal of the role of the educational system in advanced industrial societies.

## Education as an economic investment

Social scientists investigating the links between investment in education and economic productivity have encountered problems in establishing direct relationships between educational investment and economic growth, in particular in attempting to separate out the investment and consumption effects of education. Some economists have radically challenged prevailing views; for example, Berg (1973) has suggested from a review of studies that within a wide range of jobs there are few signs that the better educated workers are economically more productive. Instead he claims that college graduates are less satisfied, less controllable and less productive in jobs with a low-skill level than workers without a higher education. By arguing that educational qualifications came to be used as a screening device which functions to confine large numbers of people to low-skill, no opportunity jobs, Berg challenges the whole basis of the expansion of secondary and higher education which has taken place in advanced industrial societies. The idea that educational qualifications are technically functional has also been contested by Collins (1971 and 1975). He disputes the views that education provides the specific skills and/or general capabilities that are required for employment and that educational requirements for jobs tend to rise as technological change steadily creates a need for more highly skilled workers. He proposes a status conflict theory which sees formal education socializing individuals and conferring élite status or respect for élite status. According to this theory, rising educational requirements for employment are a result of the competition among status groups who use education to dominate the job market by imposing their cultural standards on the occupational selection process. This theory suggests that credentials are more a mark of membership in a particular status group than proof of technical skill or achievement. What one learns in schools is essentially an esoteric rhetoric to keep outsiders at arm's length.

A fundamental challenge to the proposed new role of schooling came with the publication of the 1966 Equality of Educational Opportunity Survey (EEOS) conducted by Coleman. EEOS showed that differences in existing school inputs made relatively small differences in school outputs. The debate continued with the study by Jencks and his co-authors entitled *Inequality: A Reassessment of the Effect of Family and Schooling in America* (1972). The study concluded that neither family background, occupational status, cognitive skills nor educational attainment explained much of the variations in men's individual incomes. In a controversial analysis Jencks and his associates concluded that economic success was largely the product of luck and peculiar competencies (e.g. the ability to pitch or hit a baseball) over which the government has no control. What Jencks and his associates are challenging is the belief that equalizing opportunities through schooling

23

will produce equality of income among individuals. They believe that if equality in income is required, then action should concentrate more on the redistribution of unequal income and wealth by progressive taxation.

## Education and social justice

As we have seen, it was widely assumed that as education expanded, the effect would be to produce more equality of opportunity. However, as Little and Westergaard (1964, p. 308) pointed out as early as 1964, widening of educational provision does not, by itself, reduce social inequalities in educational opportunity; it does so only if the expanded facilities are made proportionately more available to those children previously least able to take advantage of them. Studies throughout this period have continued to show that education in Britain has remained predominantly an avenue for the stable transmission of status from one generation to another. In a recent attempt to evaluate the effects of the educational expansion of the 1960s Westergaard and Resler point out that there has been no major redistribution of opportunities between children of different classes. For example, in the early 1970s manual workers' children were still less likely to enter a university than children of 'professional and technical' fathers by a factor of nearly nine times. Indeed, one ironical feature of 'comprehensive re-organization designed in part to reduce class barriers to educational opportunity [is] that the effects of these barriers became obscured from view' (Westergaard and Resler, 1975, p. 322).

## Innovation in education

The contrast between the heady optimism of the 1960s, 'an arcadian era of wonderful simplicity' and the realism of the 1970s, along with the re-emergence of emphasis on the role of heredity in educational achievement have led some commentators to claim that we have reached the end of another period of educational innovation. Warnings have recently been given that innovations can be bandwagons or hearses (Nisbet, 1975) and it has been suggested that schools must learn not only how to adopt innovations but also how to reject them (Harris *et al.*, 1975). Questions have been raised again as to whether change in education is cyclical or cumulative and proponents of innovation are talking of building structures so that innovation can be self-renewing.

Social scientists have played a further part in this loss of confidence by raising questions about how far particular educational reforms were reaching their objectives. In this country, for example, Ford (1969) has questioned the degree to which comprehensive schools can achieve the 'meritocratic' objectives of those who proposed them and Barker-Lunn (1970) has shown that change from a streamed to an unstreamed primary school structure does not transform the educational performance of working-class children. Running through the criticisms has been the central theme that schools have been asked to fulfil impossible goals; goals which require fundamental social reform rather than the sort of tinkering that educational change has represented.

In the last few years innovations in education, particularly those which claim to bring about radical change, have come increasingly under attack. The political right, the traditional opponents of radical change in education, have continued to point to the connection between progressive classroom practices and what are claimed to be falling standards in literacy, numeracy and general attainment. A major theme running through their arguments has been that progressive education does not meet the 'demands' of advanced industrial society. In the Foreword to the 1975 Black Paper on Education it was argued that 'If the non-competitive ethos of progressive education is allowed to dominate our schools we shall produce a generation unable to maintain our standards of living when opposed by fierce rivalry from overseas competitors' (Cox and Boyson, 1975, p. 1). One of the main points running through the 'Great Debate' on education has been a concern with the methods and aims of informal instruction, methods of teaching 'which seem to produce excellent results when they are in well qualified hands but are much more dubious when they are not' (Callaghan, 1976).

## The radical attack on innovation

Paradoxically, at the same time, progressive state education has come under attack from radicals who have argued that progressive schooling has developed precisely because it does meet the 'demands' of society. (This point is made by Hargreaves, 1977, p. 1.) The radical attack on innovation has set approaches to educational innovation firmly within the political context of liberalism. They suggest that the basic outlook of liberals is that, insofar as any reform is possible, it is possible within the present system, and can be achieved through enlightened social policy. They also claim that liberals have treated troublesome social problems originating in the economy as aberrations which may be alleviated by means of social programmes. Two areas, particularly, stand out as important in this strategy – education and governmental intervention in economic life. Thus the rhetoric of educational reform is seen as a smokescreen for not undertaking the economic and political reform necessary to produce a new society. Education becomes treated as a 'waste-paper basket' for dealing with society's problems – a danger well illustrated by Jencks's comments on American poverty programmes of the 1960s. 'People thought we should do a whole range of different things and slowly but surely most of the things other than educational programmes of various kinds were eroded away and more and more people began to look at the schools as the solution to all kinds of other problems' (Robinson, 1972, p. 257). So in a similar way to other critics this group are questioning the extent to which the educational system can bring about what they see as real change in society. Claiming that liberal educational reform and the social theories on which such reform is based rest upon an incomplete understanding of the economic system, they state that 'a less repressive educational system will produce little more than the "job blues" unless it can make an impact upon the nature of work and the control over production' (Bowles and Gintis, 1976, p. 49).

This point of view has been most systematically developed by a group of Marxist critics who argue that schooling has been a crucial tool for perpetuating the capitalist system amidst rapid economic change. In an attempt to revise prevailing conceptions of American educational history, these critics have interpreted the history of social reform 'less as a story of an enlightened but sadly unsuccessful corrective and more as an integral part of the process of capitalist growth itself' (Bowles and Gintis, 1976, p. 49). Whereas previously some Marxist historians tended to see the working class, or more usually working-class organizations, as continuously active agents in educational change and capitalists as generally hostile to developments in state education, the 're-visionist' educational historians still see the workers struggling for education for their children but now, by controlling decision-making in education, the ruling class are viewed as maintaining the social relations of production while ameliorating conditions and dampening conflict. From this perspective the student of the process of educational reform must consider the shifting arenas of class conflict and the mechanisms which the capitalist class has developed to mediate and deflect class conflict. Periodically, when schools cease to correspond with the structure of production, major shifts in the scope and structure of education take place, dominated in the final analysis by the class that has set the agendas of decision.

From such a viewpoint any attempt to bring about change through schooling is likely to be viewed suspiciously. As Bowles and Gintis note, after pointing out the critical role of schooling in reproducing the economic order, it is precisely this role of schooling which both 'offers the opportunity for using schools to promote revolutionary change and, at the same time, presents the danger of co-optation and assimilation into a counter-strategy to stabilize the social order' (Bowles and Gintis, 1976, p. 246). Thus while it is recognized that open classrooms and free schools, for example, might make a substantial contribution to a more liberating process of human development, the fear is that the lack of an adequate awareness on the part of the innovators of the school's place in an economic and social context may lead to a process whereby the school system accommodates and thus deflects away thrusts at its foundations. This is explicitly stated in relation to the open classroom which, it is claimed, 'was quickly perceived by liberal educators as a means of accommodating and circumscribing the growing anti-authoritarianism of young people and keeping things from getting out of hand' (Bowles and Gintis, 1976, p. 5). They clearly fear that the open classroom and the free school 'shorn of its radical rhetoric could play an important part in providing employers with workers with a "built-in" supervisor' (Bowles and Gintis, 1976, p. 13).

# Education and social control

Sharp and Green (1975) in their book *Education and Social Control* develop somewhat similar arguments in a recent case study of the infants department of a junior mixed and infants school opened in the late 1960s on a large new local authority housing estate. The authors look in detail at the classroom practices of three infant schoolteachers at Mapledene School in terms of their consciously held educational theories and attempt '. . . to study and demonstrate some of the more or less subtle ways in which the social structural "forces" impinge upon or influence the pedagogy and other social processes at the classroom and school levels' (Sharp and Green, 1975, p. vii). The typical child-centred teacher's account sees the children as having inner potentials which develop in stages. 'Readiness' is indicated by 'interest' and 'interest' in turn is shown by 'choice' in a stimulating environment. Though the regime is presented as *laissez-faire* and the children are encouraged to 'choose for themselves' the teacher does operate with a notion of hierarchy with regard to the available opportunities (particularly the work–play dichotomy). If the expected developmental stages fail to appear, the pupils' home background is very firmly blamed. While the children are seen as deprived materially, it is their 'emotional deprivation' which is most important for the teachers. The life-style of the parents is seen as producing pathological psychological traits in the children and the responsibility for this situation lies squarely with the parents themselves. The teachers faced with such 'problem children' believed that the children should play out their problems in a secure and therapeutic environment without feeling threatened. They would not 'force' or 'make' the child do the activities he seemed unwilling to do, even where his achievement was poor, because to do so would violate the integrity of the child. If, for example, a particular child spends more time than normal playing in the Wendy House this is perceived as enabling the child to act out or work through its emotional problems stemming from home. Relying on the optimism implied in the notion of 'needs' the teacher believes the child will come round when he is 'ready'. The teacher is thus enabled to integrate the 'problem' child into her practice for he can now legitimately be left alone to work through his problems, to pursue 'what interests him according to his needs'. However, this is the beginning of the process of hierarchical differentiation of the pupils. So, for example, the problem child has little contact with the teacher, is unlikely to change his 'deviant' image and this is now constantly reinforced by the acceptance of other teachers, parents and social workers.

What Sharp and Green are stressing is that though the teachers' 'accounts' give an impression of an environment with minimal control being exercised by the teacher over the pupils, in fact there is considerable direction and control over pupils in their acquisition of knowledge. Though to the teacher there is an unpatterned distribution of knowledge among the children, because each child is essentially an idiosyncratic phenomenon, there is, in fact, a pattern and structure to it, and the teachers are a key element in it, despite their generally passive self-image.

Yet it must be recognized that the case study is essentially exploratory and the authors admit that none of their propositions has been positively verified. In particular, little evidence is provided for the statements made about the relationship between the teachers' 'accounts' and the distribution of teachers' time in the infant school classrooms. Clearly the claims made warrant more systematic exploration. Similarly, extensions of this type of analysis in 'progressive' infant schools in other types of 'catchment' areas would appear important. For example, Becker (1952) found in his interviews with female, Chicago elementary schoolteachers that lower-class and upper middle-class children were considered to be the most unrewarding to teach. It would be interesting to compare teachers' 'accounts' across these two different catchment areas. Impressions suggest that the same model of emotional deprivation might occur but one that sees the child's 'pathological' characteristics as intimately connected with the crass materialism of affluent suburbia.

In a more general analysis of the progressive child-centred movement, Sharp and Green view it as impelled by a moral rhetoric which seeks to re-establish the rights of the individual for freedom, self-development and individual expression, over and above the demands of the society. It is claimed that supporters of this movement have failed to comprehend that the realities of a stratified society necessarily involve the unequal distribution of facilities, prestige and rewards. This leads Sharp and Green to view modern child-centred education as an aspect of romantic radical conservatism and to argue that the progressive educator is 'little more than an unwilling apologist of the system and his utopian solutions [are] ineffective' (Sharp and Green, 1975, p. 226). They interpret the development of progressivism in education as intimately connected with the 'demands' of society. The rigid hierarchical notion of fixed abilities is seen as incompatible with the requirement for the maximization of skilled and trained personnel and, at the same time, 'there is a need to socially structure over-optimistic aspirations as a result of the disjuncture between the mass demand for educational provision and educational opportunities available' (Sharp and Green, 1975, p. 224). Progressivism and its institutional supports are seen as particularly appropriate to the 'needs' of advanced industrial societies because of their more pervasive techniques of social control. Other sociologists have attempted to elaborate this type of analysis (e.g. Hargreaves, 1976). The growth of progressivism in the 1960s is seen as linked to changes in the relations of production; to the expansion of white-collar labour, the call for a new economic man characterized by adaptability and co-operation rather than individually competitive work relationships and the need for a major segment of the work force to be motivated by internalized norms. In the current period of economic recession it is claimed the emphasis is switching to the development of the forces of production (to which end an increasing stress is being laid upon the need for schools to inculcate basic skills in the future work force).

Based on very little evidence, on what appear strained distinctions between the forces and social relations of production, such analyses are little more than sketches. We know very little about the 'corporate and political leaders' in the USA who are seen by Bowles and Gintis as entering into a coalition with free school 'radicals'. What sectors of the economy were the corporate leaders connected with? Where do such supporters of progressivism derive from in the British situation? Why does change appear to be more marked in the primary than secondary schools? Have such corporate and political leaders been concerned about the process of change in the primary school? Furthermore, if we are going to move beyond a crude functionalism we need to know how 'the demands of society' are articulated into the classroom. This takes us back to many of the problems that 'traditional' sociologists of education were posing (Floud and Halsey, 1961). Questions about the 'autonomy' of the educational system must be raised and the possibility that the educational system, or differing parts of it, have differing degrees of 'autonomy' in different economic situations must be considered. Just as much as education can act as the 'waste-paper basket' for society's problems, so, for various groups, can it not also act as a scapegoat'?

# 3

# The extent
# and the nature
# of the change

The perpetual debate about the 'crisis in education' and the continuous heralding of the 'new educational revolution' have obscured fundamental questions such as what, if anything, is changing and in what direction is it moving. Lortie's observation in relation to the USA that 'it is paradoxical that although in recent years millions have been spent on educational development, the quality and quantity of reporting on school activities remains seriously inadequate' (Lortie, 1975, p. 214) seems equally applicable to Great Britain. The problem for students of innovation is that they cannot begin from a basis of studies in classroom observation; they cannot even state that in classrooms of such and such a kind, the pupils and teachers habitually spend the time in certain ways. Similar difficulties arise if one turns to the history of education for a discussion of change in school activities. In 1965 Cremin noted two characteristics of the contemporary history of education; first, it was predominantly a history of ideas and, second that most history was viewed from the top of the educational hierarchy. As Clifford (1973, p. 4) has pointed out:

this tendency of educational history to omit school culture is particularly misleading when the telling deals with the more 'progressive' parts of the story i.e. with change. Hence the chronicler specifies the charges against the formerly tyrannical schools, illustrates the pedagogical sins of the old fashioned teacher, paints an outline of the 'bad old schooldays'. The detailing of reformed practices, however, is sketchy and change is reducible mostly to statements of ideals'.

The varying national styles raise further problems for the observer attempting to judge the extent and the nature of the change taking place. In highly centralized systems it is difficult to know how the change is being implemented at the local level (Wylie, 1957) whereas in systems which encourage the autonomy of the school and the teacher it is frequently difficult to distinguish between the educational rhetoric and the educational practice.

## Progressive education and the inter-war years

The problems for the observer are magnified by the tendency of supporters of educational change, consciously or not, to create and sustain myths about the extent and the nature of the change taking place. This can be seen from Selleck's (1972) study of the effect of 'progressive education' on the primary school in the inter-war period which shows how 'progressive ideas' in education, which were a barely respectable doctrine held only by a group of outsiders in 1914, captured the allegiance of the opinion-makers and had by the outbreak of the Second World War become the intellectual orthodoxy. Although the main channels of opinion formation increasingly reflected the views of the 'progressives', how far any actual transformation had occurred within the classroom is much more obscure. Prior to the advent of systematic studies in the classroom, the impact of 'progressive' ideas on the classroom teacher is difficult to assess but the educational climate can be judged from a consideration of the most popular of the new experiments proposed in education – the Dalton Plan. This Plan allowed practical expression to many of the progressives' demands: individuality, freedom, an increase in social co-operation and self-government and the breaking down of the barriers be-

33

tween the subjects in the curriculum. Yet we find that the Plan's undoubted popularity – W. O. Lester Smith (1957 p. 60) recollects 'the sudden arrival here from the USA of the Dalton Plan, and the astonishing vogue that it had' – was not due simply to a desire to put progressive ideas into practice. Selleck claims that 'to a teacher who was worried that the progressives were calling into question the procedures which once had guaranteed him security, the Dalton Plan had a particular attraction. It offered a methodology – a set of procedures, ways of organizing a classroom and conducting discussion. To adopt it, or even go through the motions of adopting it, meant a certain immunity from criticism, for one could be mistaken for a reformer' (Selleck, 1972, p. 153). To the teacher who implemented the Dalton Plan it offered security at a time when change was in the air, yet it was not too far removed from what had gone before. Descriptions of schools operating the Dalton Plan suggest that after a period of trial schools settled down to a mode of work and organization which included the essential features of the plan but tempered by a varying admixture of the conventional methods of instruction. The Plan was ambiguous enough to allow most advocates to argue that the teacher should exercise less authority and allow the children to direct their own investigations while in practice, and sometimes in the writings of the Daltonians, the teacher assumed a more familiar and more powerful role.

## Pseudo-innovation

Disseminators of innovation have labelled this pseudo-innovation and seen such means of repelling would-be reformers as 'irrelevant action' (Schon, 1973). Such writing, however, often contains an underlying assumption of the objectivity of the innovation. Esland has noted that many definitions represent an innovation as a structural entity without reference to the different meanings and significance which it has for the individuals who experience it. From this standpoint, innovation is considered as if it were independent of the human interaction which creates, defines and sustains it, and through which its meaning is collectively negotiated. This is to reify innovation (Esland, 1972, p. 106). What Esland is stressing here is that innovations in education do not exist in any unchanging, objective sense but are constantly being defined, changed and redefined as a result of experience. At any one point in time different people may have quite different perceptions of an innovation and over time the same person may change his perceptions of an innovation.

This can be illustrated by Shipman's *et al.*'s (1974) study of the Keele Integrated Studies Project. He notes that, despite the fact that the three related elements in the role expected of teachers who were involved in the innovation: subject integration, use of enquiry methods and membership of a team, were spelled out in a number of documents for schools as well as being explained by co-ordinators and at conferences, in practice no broad agreement on the underlying objectives and definitions of the role of the teachers was shared by the parties involved. The explanation seemed to lie in the different perspectives held by the workers on the Project, the schools and the local education authorities. However close the contact between them, they were each primarily concerned with a different set of problems and each saw the innovation as a means of achieving a different set of objectives. While the objectives of the Project Team centred on the need to obtain the co-operation to test a new approach to both content and method, the local advisory staff of the education authorities accepted the objectives of the Project as legitimate but in practice were more concerned with the relevance of the innovation to the problems faced by subject teachers in the humanities and with the maintenance and raising of standards of attainment in the schools. Between these two in-fluences were the teachers who were mainly concerned with the immediate problems of the classroom. To them the Project offered materials that would help introduce new courses that seemed to be educationally desirable and liable to motivate children more than traditional subject teaching. They were less concerned with the underlying philosophies of integration than the Project Team and less concerned with adopting new forms of team teaching. They were concerned with the concrete problems of motivation, discipline, and the maintenance and assessment of work. Shipman emphasizes, however, that it is not just that the various parties involved adopt their own versions of the innovation and work it towards their own ends. Each of the parties over the course of time changed their position. Teachers, for example, were subject to many differing influences on their role from inside the school and interviews showed many diverse attitudes even among teachers in the same school.

## The new primary education

A similar problem of distinguishing between educational rhetoric and educational practice arose in the 1960s when the world looked to England as the home of the 'new primary education'. During this period the educational opinion-makers were almost unanimously in favour of the new primary school. The ubiquitous visitor from Mars locked away in a library with copies of educational periodicals of the last decade and subsequently released to visit schools would soon be in a state of confusion at the great divide between what educationists have argued should be done and what many teachers continue to do.

The Plowden Report *Children and their Primary Schools*, published in 1967, judged the extent of change from the estimate of Her Majesty's Inspectors of Schools who were thought to be in the best position to give a comprehensive report on what was going on in the primary schools in England and Wales. Commentators on the Plowden Report have judged it successful in its evangelical purpose of reinforcing and strengthening the 'liberating' effects of progressive education in a large number of schools. However, as research as opposed to informed impression has become available questions have been raised about how much change has in fact taken place. Barker-Lunn's (1970) study of *Streaming in the Primary School* suggested that only about half the staff in non-streamed schools could be called 'non-streamers'. The others held attitudes more typical of teachers in streamed schools appearing to create a 'streamed atmosphere' within their non-streamed classes; streaming their children so that different ability groups were seated in different parts of the classroom. Their teaching methods, their lessons and their attitudes tended to reflect the pattern found in streamed schools.

Bennett and Jordan's (1975 and 1976) descriptive study of the teaching styles of a large sample of junior school teachers in the north-west of England is one of the few empirical attempts to look at what goes on behind the classroom door in this country. They were interested in how far the type of progressive primary school practice promoted by the Plowden Report existed in practice; for example, how far pupils could choose their own activities in the classrooms and how far teachers were now adopting a consultative, guiding and stimulating tone rather than a didactic one. Bennett and Jordan concluded that most teachers adopt mixed strategies of teaching, using informal and formal strategies in different degrees; only about one teacher in six could be said to be teaching informally. On particular areas of teaching style they found in relation to classroom management, for example, that most teachers still sit their pupils separately or in pairs rather than in larger groups and that the pupils remain in the same seat for most activities. On teacher's organization of work in their class it was found that individual work was more favoured than group work and that the proportion of time set aside for work chosen by pupils was much less than that for teacher-chosen tasks.

Criticism has been made that this survey of the north-west was not an accurate reflection of the national picture but the report of the Plowden Committee (1967) reported little regional variation and Boydell's (1971) research reported relatively similar findings to Bennett and Jordan's from a survey of the structure of junior school classrooms in the city and county of Leicester. Further criticism has been expressed that the questionnaire method used in this survey was not the most appropriate method for the measurement of teaching style. Clearly there are difficulties in self-reporting, and these will be referred to later, but in this study an attempt was made by the research team and the local education authority primary advisers to confirm the validity of the findings by observation and in general they found teachers gave an accurate description of their teaching in their responses.

## The nature of the change

Besides myths arising as to the extent of the change, they may also arise as to the nature of the change. This can be clearly seen from an examination of books and articles (Silberman, 1970; Psaltis, 1972) on the subject of English primary schools intended for an American audience interested in the question of open education. These books approximate to the 'popular sociology' described by Chinoy (1964) in that while they deal with many of the questions that concern social scientists, they are unconstrained by scholarly canons and are explicitly directed towards a 'popular' or mass audience. This type of writing falls somewhere between journalism and scholarly writing, being based mainly on journalistic observations made during a limited number of visits to carefully selected schools, it is exaggerated and fails to distinguish the trivial from the consequential. However, although their contributions to understanding may be limited, these works are important in their influence. They resulted in particular images of English primary schools, especially the schools of Leicestershire and Oxfordshire, becoming the symbol of hope for many American school reformers of the 1960s and the 1970s and led to the frequent pilgrimages by American educationists during this period.

Silberman (1970) in *Crisis in the Classroom*, a book which it is asserted had a tremendous impact on elementary schools in the USA, presents a picture of English primary schools largely in terms of items, most of which exemplify how children are 'intrinsically' motivated, make their own choices about what they should learn, set their own standards, move about in the classroom without apparent external controls and, within this free atmosphere, achieve high standards of academic and artistic performance. He claims that '. . . in every formal classroom that I went to visit in England, children were restless, were whispering to one another when the teacher was not looking, were ignoring the lesson or baiting the teacher or annoying other children' while in the schools organized on the basis of informal schooling 'the joyfulness is pervasive; in almost every classroom visited, virtually every child appeared happy and engaged. One simply does not see bored or restless or unhappy youngster, or youngsters with the glazed look'. Psaltis (1972) is an article entitled 'A humanistic experience: the British Primary Schools', a contribution to a reader written for those committing their lives and careers to changing the schools, observed that it was typical in the schools she visited for the children to choose where they wished to become engaged from a rich variety of learning experiences available in the school. The length of time a child engaged in any activity was seen to be determined by his interest, involvement and productivity around a particular task, rather than by predetermined bell-controlled periods.

Puzzled by these accounts of a mass schooling virtually free of conflict and coercion and the failure of competent experienced teachers to implement open education in the Silberman fashion, researchers have engaged in more detailed study of the day-to-day occurrences in English primary schools. Employing the methodology of participant observation rather than the more systematic observation of Bennett and Boydell, Berlak *et al.* (1975) looked in detail at several informal primary schools in Leicester and Leicestershire. They found that the language of freedom, self-motivation and child-set standards commonly used to characterize these schools did not capture the complexities of the actual schooling. In no school they studied did a child have the choice not to learn to read or do mathematics and there were virtually no instances of children being allowed to do nothing. The teachers did not subscribe, as commonly portrayed, to a particular set of educational beliefs but mirrored society in their contrary notions about the proper way children should be reared, what is success and how it is pursued in the society, what traditions are precious and need to be sustained, what is a just allocation of the resources of the society, and similar issues.

The picture that is presented is one of schooling as a set of persisting dilemmas and it is the teacher in each classroom who resolves these conflicting claims. In their paper the authors address themselves to the teachers' patterns of resolution of three such dilemmas: teacher making learning decisions for children versus children making learning decisions, intrinsic versus extrinsic motivation, and teacher setting and maintaining standards for children's learning and development versus children setting their own standards. The complex realities of informal education are captured in this description of the work of a teacher in a Leicester primary school.

In a primary school in one of the poorer sections of Leicester, Mrs Lawton teaches twenty-five 7-year-olds. The morning is devoted primarily to work in the 'basics' – reading, maths and writing – with a brief interruption for assembly. Mrs Lawton sets daily minimum work expectations; everyone will write a story, all but the strongest readers will read individually to the teacher or the head, and each will do a given maths task. Moreover, each child works with a small group at his maths and his story at a specified time. During a work period, Mrs Lawton may tell one child to write a longer story, more often than not ignoring a child's apparent reluctance, but may be satisfied with a shorter story from another child. When a child has finished the required work, or if no work is required at a given time generally in the afternoons, he may 'choose' from activities such as reading corner, painting, Wendy house, or blocks. At such times, one might see three children in 'dress-ups' wheeling a carriage across the playground unbeknown to the teacher, who might be 'hearing' the last of her students read. (Berlak *et al.*, 1975, p. 226)

In relation to the first dilemma of teacher making learning decisions for children versus children making learning decisions, Mrs Lawton claims that children 'need freedom but also guidance' (Berlak, 1975, p. 228). She resolves the dilemma by making all the decisions on whether or not a child will study in a given area and most of the decisions about what is to be learned, when the task is to begin and when it is to be completed and how the learner is to proceed with the task in the 'basics' – reading, writing and maths. She leaves most decisions in the non-basics to the children 'I direct them, but I give them choice as well. Especially with "activities" and creative work, I allow them to choose more than written work' (Berlak, 1975, p. 228). Such descriptions of the teacher's resolution of these dilemma fits more closely with what is known of the primary school teacher's wider world views. A general survey of the political views of teachers in different educational institutions during the British General Election of 1974 (National Opinion Poll, 1974) showed that the primary school was the type of educational institution where the staff had the highest intention to vote Conservative (44 per cent against the total sample intention of 37 per cent). In terms of staff educational attitudes the primary school was the type of educational institution where the staff were least likely to agree with the elimination of the grammar schools. Only 18 per cent were for their elimination compared with the total teacher sample of 24 per cent. It is difficult to match much of the writing on the 'new primary education' with the above information.

Furthermore, it is increasingly unclear how far the perpetuation of myths contained in much popular writing is in the interests of the promoters of educational change. As we shall see, accounts of attempts to implement open education in the USA abound with descriptions of competent teachers feeling frustrated because they could not implement the English model as they understood it. Children were not making wise decisions about their learning, staying with a task long enough to complete it satisfactorily, or exhibiting the joy of self-motivated study. The feeling of frustration generated led in many cases to a rapid abandonment of attempts to implement the innovations. Explanations of this problem have usually been put forward in terms of the difficulties of transplanting ideas from one society to another and the need for more long-term professional education of American teachers to develop their autonomy. At least an equally satisfactory alternative explanation is that the promoters of educational change supported a literature which provided the teachers with inadequate or misleading ideas. The utopian claims which educational promoters put forward may be useful in the generation and diffusion of interest in a new set of ideas but may be extremely dysfunctional in the implementation process.

This may in part explain the findings of Goodlad *et al.*'s (1970) study of elementary school in the USA, *Behind the Classroom Door*. Drawing on a detailed investigation of 150 classrooms from Kindergarten to grade three in twenty-six urban school districts across the USA, Goodlad concluded that few of the most widely recommended educational ideas and practices have found their way into the classroom. For example, despite recent curricular reform, teaching was predominantly telling and questioning by the teacher, with children responding one by one or occasionally in chorus. A considerable discrepancy was found between the teacher's perceptions of his or her own innovative behaviour and the perceptions of observers. The teachers in Goodlad *et al.*'s study thought they were individualizing instruction, encouraging inductive learning, etc. – but with few people in the school having any knowledge of the innovation, let alone having seen it in practice, there were clear problems in implementation. These problems have led Goodlad to stress that 'it is essential that educational change begins from a full understanding of what already exists'.

In this chapter an exploration has been made of some of the myths, surrounding the style, extent and nature of educational change in this country. The material examined has been largely drawn from the primary school but similar material relating to the secondary school could readily have been presented (see, for example, Taylor, 1963; Eggleston *et al.*, 1976). Eggleston *et al.* (1976) carried out research concerned to identify the processes of science teaching, i.e. the combination of a particular set of learning experiences which might constitute a method of teaching, and then to investigate possible relationships between such methods and the products of the teaching, i.e. the attitudes and attainment levels of the students. The research formed part of the Schools Council Project for the Evaluation of Science Teaching Methods and was carried out at a time when 'Nuffield Science' was well established in secondary schools in England and Wales. The 'Nuffield approach' aimed at more than a mere revamping of course content. While each separate curriculum, biology, chemistry and physics had its own philosophy embodied in a statement of aims, the common theme developed by all of them was to move away from the teaching of science in the schools as a set of received facts and principles towards a greater participation of students in the exploration of novel ideas. From observations of more than a hundred teachers of biology, chemistry and physics, giving three to four hundred lessons between them, the picture to emerge contrasted with that expected in the wake of Nuffield. For example, over a quarter of the teachers observed never encouraged the designing of experiments through their questioning and a significant proportion never questioned their students' powers of observation during practical work.

An underlying assumption has been that educational innovation is more likely to succeed if the myths surrounding educational change are stripped away and the problems in implementing change in schools squarely faced. In this country there is a danger that the myth of teacher autonomy has lulled many concerned with the promoting of innovation into a state of complacency and even into an erroneous view that innovation has already been achieved. Marshall asserts that the 'primary school

42

revolution' came about because 'teachers in infant classes began to act on professional instinct that told them a happy child actively involved on something he wanted to do was getting more out of his educational opportunities than a passive bored child politely resisting most of the instructions dished out to him in 30 minute parcels' (Marshall, 1970). However, this belief in the inherent ability of teachers to work their correct course (a course which Miss Marshall would approve) does not appear to coincide with systematic descriptions of what teachers actually do in primary and secondary schools. If, as the promoters hope, there is to be successful implementation of change in this country, if the divide between rhetoric and reality is to be bridged, if change is not to be blunted on the school and classroom door, developments in our description and understanding of what goes on in schools must be made.

# 4

# The prospect
# of planned
# social change

In the last chapter it was pointed out how there is often a gap between *myths* surrounding the nature and extent of an educational
change and its *actual* nature and extent. An analysis of the literature on educational change shows that much of it is concerned
with ways of effecting changes in education, particularly how to
bring about the required transformation in its major practitioners,
the teachers. In this chapter a critical examination will be made of
the various strategies suggested for bringing about such changes.
Such strategies were often based on the work of social scientists
who believed that in the new technological society social planning
would play a key role. It was hoped that the developments in economic planning post-Keynes heralded the beginnings of more
systematic attempts among social scientists to understand and
plan social change.

Advances in this area were made during the Second World War
when social scientists moved into positions where they were increasingly involved with practical problems and, in particular,
how to implement and control the change process. A new optimism arose among some researchers that they could employ the

methods of social science to solve problems of vital significance to society. An eminent social psychologist's view was that 'One of the by-products of the Second World War of which society is hardly aware is the new stage of development which the social sciences have reached. This development may indeed prove as revolutionary as the atom bomb' (Lewin, 1952, p. 188). He further argued that although the social sciences might still be in their infancy compared to other sciences, they already knew enough to intervene in social problems and to bring about changes with some success. Lewin and his followers had a view of a society where the tendency was towards change and where the two major ideas systems relating to the methods to be employed in controlling and directing forces in change – the law of non-intervention and the law of radical intervention – were directly opposed. To fill this gap they developed the notion of planned change – a method which employs social technology – to help solve the problems, as the only feasible alternative within a liberal democratic society. Schein has recently summarized the aspirations of the proponents of planned change in relation to education 'We do not have to, in relation to education, rely on the slow process of evolution, nor would it be appropriate or desirable, to have a more drastic revolutionary kind of educational reform. We seek a process that lies between these two extremes . . .' (Schein, 1972, p. 75).

## Strategies of change

As interest in this area began to develop, workers in the field doubted whether the traditional strategies for bringing about change were effective. In order to point up their criticisms of earlier strategies writers isolated three broad strategies of educational change, each of which is rooted in a particular image of the practitioner (Sieber, 1972; Bennis et al., 1969). Each type implies a distinctive strategy for effecting change; in terms of different foci for change, different channels of influence and different types of change agent. This is not meant to imply that all strategies of change are included in this list. (For a fuller discussion see Tichy, 1975.) In Table 1 an adaptation of the work of Bennis et al. (1969) and Sieber (1972) shows the three major strategies.

It is argued here that all efforts to induce change employ a

*Table 1  Strategies for inducing educational change*

|  | Image of the practitioner | Locus of change | Channel of influence | Change agent |
| --- | --- | --- | --- | --- |
| Empirical-rational | The rational man | Internal-intellective | One-way communication | Lecturer, writer, educational critic |
| Power-coercive | The powerless functionary | External-structural | Prescriptions and sanctions (orders, laws, regulations) | Legislator, adminstrator, pressure group |
| Normative Re-educational | The co-operator | Internal-affective (attitudinal) | Two-way communication | Consultant, human relations expert |

combination of these strategies, e.g. many innovations employ both power-coercive and empirical rational strategies. While these categories are useful for the purposes of analysis, they are, of course, inevitably somewhat arbitrary and rarely exist in a pure form.

## Empirical-rational

This first change strategy is rooted in the image of the practitioner as a rational man. The change process is seen as essentially concerned with the teacher gaining awareness and understanding of innovations – the teacher as a rational man only needs to be informed and he will change his mind. The underlying assumption is that reason determines the process of initiating innovations and that scientific investigation is the best means of extending knowledge, from the initial basic research to the final practical application. Sieber points out that one set of drawbacks of this strategy is that by implication the teacher is seen as

> invulnerable to the opinions of his associates, the values to which he has been exposed as an occupant of antecedent statuses (such as social class or community of origin), the ideologies of his occupational group, or any features of his environment that ordinarily place constraints on goal-oriented behaviours. In short, he is omnipotent and selfless, and the only barrier to his optimal functioning is *ignorance*. (Sieber, 1972, p. 364)

Furthermore, this strategy of change relies on the development of a high level of consensus within a society on the need for a given form of change. Those involved in planning and change have often neglected to see that many people in school settings do not seek change or react enthusiastically to it. In Britain attempts to introduce curriculum change have often been based on the assumption that a significant proportion of teachers were agreed as to the necessity for change, were willing to change and have the time and energy to change. It has been suggested, for example, that one problem facing the Schools Council is that it 'blandly assumes an innovative climate on the basis of little or no evidence. That some teachers and some schools have experimented with new approaches cannot be doubted; that others would do so if helped is more than likely; but whether the majority see the necessity or can make the effort is not proven' (Richards, 1974, p. 326).

Even the teacher oriented to change and attempting to base his decisions on the best available information is faced with problems. Besides having to work within the constraints of the 'teacher's day' (Hilsum and Cane, 1971) he is also faced by the frequently conflicting advice of experts who employ increasingly sophisticated research methods. While it is important to avoid simplistic assumptions in evaluating the actual and likely pay-offs from educational research, research conducted into teachers' attitudes towards and perceptions of educational research and change clearly show the problems. For example, Cane and Schroeder (1970) found that more than half the assistant teachers in the schools they sampled were completely unfamiliar with the works of eleven out of fourteen prominent educational researchers listed in their questionnaire. Only 30–50 per cent of the assistant teachers knew of the publications of the Schools Council and the National Foundation for Educational Research. While recent attempts to improve the diffusion of educational research are to be welcomed, there are likely to remain major problems for the teacher trying to base his practice on the rational evaluation of information available to him. The possible implications for research itself of a closer link between research, research workers and classroom practice have recently been explored by Taylor (1975). He suggests that 'the fact that undertaking research and theorizing involves no direct threat to accepted practice means that it can be permitted with a minimum of social constraint. If the links between research and practice were immediate and direct, there would be much more interest in controlling the process and ensuring some kind of doctrinal uniformity' (Taylor, 1975, p. 225).

## Power-coercive

Power-coercive strategies were historically the best-known ways in which educational systems have been developed and regulated and were often a clear reflection of a historical and social climate where authoritarian leadership was regarded as legitimate. In this mode change occurs by the deliberate restructuring of the situation by a superordinate having the necessary authority. This can be seen at a number of levels ranging from a government enforcing a system of comprehensive schooling to the head teacher decreeing that his school will move over from a streamed to an unstreamed form of organization. The political, legal and economic sanctions which underlie this strategy usually remain latent and the superordinate has to gain compliance by the more immediate exercise of personal influence and persuasion.

While the move away from this strategy reflects changes in the value system of the wider society it is due, also, to the increasing realization of the problems of prescribing change. A consideration of certain key features of school settings allows us to see why power does not necessarily evoke compliance, even when exercised by legally constituted bodies, and to examine obstacles to change by means of administrative or legal fiat (Sieber, 1972). First, the relative insulation of the teaching role and its consequent low visibility makes it possible for schools and teachers to deviate from regulations without being noticed. The superior's evidence of compliance usually comes from communication that flows from lower to higher echelons and information can be readily withheld, distorted or explained away. Furthermore, the existence of rules allows for the possibility of complying with the letter of the law without regard to the spirit. Sarason (1971) has pointed out how in many innovations even the question of the intended consequences has been begged. There is no explicit, objective statement of criteria by which to decide whether things are the way they ought to be. In this situation the chances of ritualistic compliance

48

that ignores the intent of the innovation must be high.

A second major set of reasons why compliance does not flow automatically is due to conflict with extra-organizational pressures, e.g. the ideology of professionalism and organizational demands and incentives. Sarason (1971) has correctly reminded us of the complexity of the teacher's task stemming from the number and diversity of children each teacher has to handle and from the pressure to adhere to a time schedule to bring children to a given level. Innovations by regulation which raise problems for teachers in these spheres or create problems of social control with the 'involuntary' clients of the schools are likely to face modifications at the school level.

Finally the environment into which an innovation is introduced will determine how the innovation will be altered and adopted. In the USA Corwin (1973) has traced how the politically volatile climate in which the Teacher Corps, a massive federal intervention programme involving several hundred universities and school systems, was operating critically affected its success. The very fact that the issues had become sufficiently political to require public legislation meant that the programme would be subjected to compromise from the start. The lack of a consensus within the society on the need for change, or the appropriate direction or vehicle for change, compromised the programme's legitimacy and integrity. Furthermore, as a corollary of the lack of consensus among the general public, there was little consensus among the constituent members of the programme. Clearly if a change is to be introduced by law there is a need for lengthy preparation of the affected parties.

*Normative re-educational*

Interest in this area began to develop as workers in the field doubted whether relying solely on rational persuasion or administrative fiat was sufficient. In particular there was a growing awareness that relying solely on rational persuasion (expert power) was insufficient because 'too often, rational elements are denied or rendered impotent because they conflict with a strongly ingrained belief, consciously or unconsciously held' (Bennis, 1966, p. 176). This led to an increased concentration on the internal states of the

49

individual and fundamentally this strategy is concerned with changing people – their perceptions, attitudes and behaviour. Thus Argyris's statement that 'the focus is on people, not because we are unconcerned about organizations but because people create and maintain organizations. Also it is people who must design, accept and implement changes that are required to keep the organization in a healthy state' (1971, p. ix) shows how this strategy concentrates on the people variable as a point of entry rather than on the goals, structure and technologies of the organization.

Lewin's early work in this field on group approaches to attitude change spoke of change as involving three steps: unfreezing, moving and freezing (Lewin, 1947, pp. 228–9) and this has been elaborated upon by Schein (1972) who uses the terms unfreezing, changing and freezing to designate the steps. The particular attention paid to Stage One – the unfreezing process and the resistance to change – is clear in Schein's statement that 'the change agent must assume that the members of the system will be committed to their present ways of operating and will, therefore, resist learning something new. As a consequence the *essence* of a planned change process is the *unlearning* of present ways of doing things. It is felt to be in this unlearning process that most of the difficulties of planned change arise' (Schein, 1972, p. 75). Writers have emphasized the problem of the change agent or management in overcoming resistance to change; believing that if change is to occur, the individual has to abandon, or at least modify old action patterns, beliefs and attitudes. The dangers of neglecting the social support necessary for normative re-education have led writers such as Miles (1964) to place great emphasis on the use of 'temporary systems' such as attendance at courses or seminars in which members are re-educated in a setting totally separated from their normal social supports. However, there is evidence which suggests that as soon as persons return to their normal settings the sanctions that controlled their former behaviour reasserted themselves. In particular, studies of the effectiveness of human relations training efforts in industry have suggested the price of ignoring the power structure of the organization and its likely effects on implementation. Tannenbaum, Weschler and Massarik note that 'One report is particularly distressing in that it points out that some people who returned from a training experience were actually "worse off" than they had been before . . . lacking the power to change (existing supervisory practices) by themselves, the trainees either returned to their old behaviours or became dissatisfied and left for employment elsewhere' (1961, pp. 222–3). It is, partly, results like these which have led to the use of a growing variety of group techniques and it is possible to envisage a continuum, ranging from the group concern with individual change through the group therapy techniques practised within organizations to the use of group methods for the solving of a specific organizational problem (Hoyle, 1970).

### Artisans rather than scientists

It is important to view such practitioners of planned social change as artisans rather than scientists (Tichy, 1974). Their approaches are based on implicit ideas rather than sets of clearly formulated principles. Underlying the different techniques utilized in the planning of change are the change agent's evaluative orientation to social change such as his attitudes towards important social changes, his own social change goals, and the goals he feels change agents should have.

So, for example, the work of many advocating the use of normative re-educational strategies was closely linked to the view they had of the type of organizations most appropriate to a rapidly changing society. At the time the most influential description of complex organizations was Weber's work on bureaucracy. Weber tried to describe the characteristics of bureaucracies that separated them from other, less formal, types of work organizations. His analysis specified (1) positions become explicitly defined *offices*; (2) the social relationships are inherently *impersonal*; (3) norms become explicit *rules and regulations*; (4) a high degree of *specialization* of function and utilization of criteria of *technical* competence; and (5) a formalized *hierarchy* of offices.

The critics argue that while the Weberian model of bureaucratic organizations was an elegant social invention, capable of organizing and co-ordinating the productive processes of the 'Industrial Revolution', it was hopelessly inadequate in the contemporary situation. In particular, they stressed the inability of this organizational model to cope with a constantly changing situa-

51

tion. (A full list of the suggested shortcomings are to be found in Bennis, 1966, p. 4.) In the critique there is an emphasis on the rigidity of the model with little or no attention paid to the rich complexity of bureaucratic organizations *in action*. As Stephenson (1975, p. 253) has pointed out, little attention is paid to the patterns of indulgence (see Gouldner, 1954), and the countless ways in which the model is modified in practice.

In its place the enthusiasts of planned change proposed a model which has been called 'The Human Relations Model', i.e. horizontal patterns of authority, low specialization, a minimum of general rules, an emphasis on personal relations, etc. Leadership and decision-making are conceptualized differently in each model. Whereas in the bureaucratic model leadership is a function of formal position in the hierarchy with its prescribed range and scope of decision-making; in the human relations model leadership is seen as informal, achieved and related to task while decisions are made collaboratively by the group who will be affected by the decisions made. As Hoyle points out, it is the human relations model which 'has provided the guiding metaphor for training experiences in management and administration, and the theoretical materials for a variety of change strategies' (Hoyle, 1975, p. 32). It is seen by those involved in such change programmes to have two great advantages: first, that it is characterized by a flexibility, adaptability and structural looseness which is regarded as 'functional' for periods of rapid change and, second, that its democratic structure and support for self-actualization is congruent with the prevailing world view.

Just as radical critics have recently suggested the need for a reanalysis of innovation in education (see Chapter 2), so their colleagues have called for a re-assessment of the relationship between social science, planning and education. The work of social scientists involved in this field has been seen as characterized by practicality (Collins, 1975, p. 14); their aim has been to achieve some concrete goal in the world. Accepting some educators' definition of a 'social problem' – the lack of change in education – they have attempted to produce policies that will reliably change the educational situation. Critics have argued that this advice usually remains rooted within the conventional wisdom of popular (especially liberal) political positions. Remaining within the narrow focus of a social problem orientation is seen as leading to a concern with the here and now of a particular problem and preventing a consideration of the wider view which might see the 'problem' as just one of a set of influences within a larger pattern of variables.

It is suggested that those involved in the planning of change in education have too readily accepted the 'conventional wisdom' of professional educator; a world view with its own brand of faith and dogma. It is the acceptance of this world view, with its twin related assumptions that education can be separated from politics and that education should be entrusted to professional experts which has underlain much writing and research on the implementation of innovation in education. It has led many to view differences in educational ideas between teachers and administrators, between teachers themselves, or between teachers and parents or children, as temporary aberrations which can easily be removed by greater contact, improvement of communications and/or 're-training' programmes. The notion that these different views might be more deeply rooted in different locations within the wider social structure and as such much less amenable to change has been less frequently explored.

The vocabulary of innovation has similarly reflected the educators' 'conventional wisdom'. Thus Bressler (1963, p. 85) has noted that in the vocabulary of unlimited hope of the educationist words such as 'conflict' and 'force' are rejected. Karier (1973, p. 86) has traced how this omission can be linked to the influence of progressive educators like Dewey who regarded all conflict as irrational and, in principle, avoidable. He has pointed out how the earlier progressives, like their latter-day counterparts 'sought social change without conflict and violence [by] placing their faith in science and technology as "creators of human values" and turning to a mass system of education that would impart these values to the children of the immigrant' (Karier, 1973, p. 106).

## A political model of organizations

Much of the work on innovation in education has tended to avoid the question of power and the political features of organizational life. From one point of view power can be seen to be relatively un-

53

problematic in bureaucratic-type organizations. It is legitimized through investing the organizational head with legal authority which he may then partially delegate through the hierarchical structure. Many of the modifications of bureaucratic structures arise out of compromises which come through *informal* power within the organization and through the power which trade unions can exercise. However within the human relations view there has, at times, been an acceptance of a unitary view of organizations and a rejection of a pluralist view. It has failed to see that much consensus occurs only after prolonged battle and that many decisions are not consensus but the prevalence of one group over another (Baldridge, 1971, p. 14). Where conflict arises, it is seen as accidental arising only out of the existence of differing personalities, failure of communication and lack of understanding. As Stephenson (1975, p. 253) points out, there is a rejection of conflict as a reflection of fundamental and genuine differences of interest.

In his consideration of universities, organizations with a very diffuse, differentiated goal system, Baldridge (1971) felt it necessary to propose a new model – the political model. It is interesting to reflect that it was partly Bennis's experience as an administrator at the State University of New York at Buffalo (Bennis, 1970) which led him to modify his approach and talk of 'potential partisans'. Baldridge's new model draws heavily on the body of theoretical thought characterized in sociology as conflict theory. He suggests that many conflict ideas proposed for the larger society can be applied to the smaller social system of an organization. In particular he stresses (Baldridge, 1971, pp. 15–16):

(i) Conflict theorists emphasize the fragmentation of interest groups, each with its own particular goals.

(ii) Conflict theorists study the interaction of these different interest groups and especially the conflict processes by which one group tries to gain advantages over another.

(iii) Interest groups cluster around divergent values, and the study of conflicting interests is a key part of the analysis.

(iv) The study of change is a central feature of the conflict approach, for change is to be expected if the social system is fragmented by divergent values and conflicting interest groups.

54

In contrast to the human relations approach to organizations which argues that many problems in organizations may be related to faulty communication and may therefore be alleviated by increased communication and consultation, this perspective contends that there are many instances of real conflict that cannot be communicated away. It is based on a more realistic view of the people involved in organizations, which recognizes man's ability to respond to situations and to alter them in ways that are significant for them. Furthermore, it recognizes that many problems arise because two sides do clearly understand each other and have the knowledge that the other's possible gain will be at their expense. Looking at innovation in this way implies that we pay particularly close attention to those involved in the planning of change. Rather than accepting their claims that they are free of any concerns outside their 'science', that they are neutral instruments rather than goal-makers, the above approach would be concerned about their ability to shape and order the lives of other men. Such an approach would explore the particular perspectives associated with the change agents and contrast these with the perspectives of other groups concerned with the change process.

## The Tavistock approach

The importance of conflict theory can be seen from a consideration of recent work in Britain. Here interest in the use of normative re-educational techniques in relation to change has been generated by, among others, the Tavistock Institute of Human Relations which was founded in 1947 by psychologists and others to undertake research, consultancy and teaching in the field of the social sciences. In a similar way to Lewin and his followers, this group believed that the techniques they had developed during their wartime experiences could be further extended and applied in industry and elsewhere (Brown, 1967). A recent attempt to utilize perspectives drawn from the Tavistock approach in relation to change in education can be found in Elizabeth Richardson's (1973) *The Teacher, the School and the Task of Management*. Richardson's work draws on two main approaches: the psychoanalytic study of human behaviour on the one side and the study of organizations as open institutions on the other. Influenced by Bion's ideas for the analysis of group phenomena, she is particularly concerned with the extent to which the unrecognized and largely unconscious feelings that teachers have about each other and their pupils may be hindering the conscious, rational efforts being made by those same teachers, as professional persons, to implement desirable changes in the system.

From 1968 to 1971, Richardson worked as consultant to the headmaster and staff of a fast expanding Somerset comprehensive school. The research is seen as collaborative in that 'the people with whom the consultant works must never be mere objects in study but always partners in study'. The collaborative role is linked to a very narrow definition of the consultant's role which involved working with the staff for three years, yet remaining technically a visitor throughout that period, 'a visitor who never observed a lesson, scarcely ever spoke with any of the pupils and never directly encountered any of the parents as parents' (Richardson, 1973, p. xiii). The reader, as well as the staff, is reliant upon a high level of expertise on the part of the consultant in making largely intuitive interpretations of their unconscious, as well as conscious, feelings, beliefs and attitudes within the staff group.

The danger here is that the consultant has only a limited perspective, not only due to her diagnostic frameworks, but also to real world constraints of time, money and access to certain information. As a result, the diagnosis may be partial; the implicit and explicit assumptions by which the consultant selects her data and in terms of which she interprets it, may divert her attention away from alternative explanations. At one level this may be acceptable but from the point of view of the staff they have access to only one 'expert'. In Richardson's work there appears at times a conscious striving for explanation in terms of subconscious and unconscious motives and an unwillingness to face up to the interpretations which challenge her own assumptions.

Let us examine some of the problems that Richardson looks at. She deals with the problem of the staff's increasing anger with the headmaster which had resulted in certain of them directly challenging the head in a staff meeting. She resolves this by noting that 'either way, the important thing to recognize is that those who were able to take the risk of challenging him in public were also expressing a growing trust in him by doing so'. When some of the staff began to complain about litter and the 'bad manners' of the pupils, the consultant, despite the nature of her role, asserts that her impression 'whenever I found myself going in or out of the buildings' was that these were not problems. The staff who were trying to force the head to adopt what Richardson considers 'a more dictatorial [sic] approach' were failing to recognize, she writes, that if they had been in a school that did have a dictatorial head they would probably have been exerting a comparable pressure to reduce the amount of direction from the top.

These comments illustrate how particular events are examined in terms of preconceived frameworks and alternative explanations appear unconsidered. At times the consultant fails to take account of man's ability to respond to situations and to alter them in ways that are *significant* for him. The discrepancy between some of the staff's and the consultant's view of significance appears to derive in large part from the consultant's view of the ideal man. The consultant is convinced that her values are right and that others must change and, as Stephenson argues, such consultancy 'comes near to selecting the "one best way" allegedly so beloved by those engaged in scientific management' (Stephenson, 1975, p. 254). In a situation where staff members have genuine disagreements about organizational tasks and role behaviour and are using the political process in the school to bring about change, the consultants themselves become part of the political process. In this way there is a possibility they might be 'used' by various groups in the change process who have similar views of the ideal organization and the ideal man. Clearly the origins of such processes of collaboration are worthy of close attention. As Collins has pointed out, even if there were a truly scientific sociology in the hands of applied sociologists it would not 'eliminate the manoeuvring over power which goes on in any organization within which different factions attempt to bolster their own positions with allegedly neutral expertise' (Collins, 1975, p. 16).

In this chapter it has been suggested that it is important to view various change strategies in terms of their underlying value orientations. Different types of change agent are likely to view the school in different ways and each type will have their own set of standards for measuring the state of the school in order to plan an intervention. It is essential, therefore, to view the planning of change in a wider context and to educate would-be consumers as to the different bases associated with different change agents. Furthermore, if different strategies are available there is a need for the evaluation of their effectiveness. This involves case studies of change, and in particular of change strategies, in operation. This will be considered in the next chapter.

# 5

# Case studies of change

In the last chapter it was argued that many theorists and practitioners in the field of planned change do not show adequate awareness of the consequences of their intervention in the change process. Relying on studies of industrial settings and their own experience, they assume that we already possess adequate descriptions of the change process in schools and colleges. Furthermore, they frequently assume a 'messianic' stance (Brubaker and Nelson, 1975, p. 65) operating under an illusion that they are manipulating others without being subject to the change process themselves. However, our lack of knowledge about the merits and demerits of various approaches and in particular of the unknown and unpredicted effects of particular change initiatives has led social scientists, particularly in the USA, to become interested in studying the actualities of the change process as distinct from what the change literature says about the process. In this they have been supported by Maslow's statement about the need for observation and reporting of educational experiments as opposed to 'retrospective stories of the programme, the faith and the confident expectations but with inadequate accounts of just what was done, how and when and of just what happened and didn't happen as a result' (Maslow, 1965, p. 13).

Books dealing with innovative schools have frequently been over-concerned with providing a single point of view rather than with examining the problems faced in the change process. This type of approach is explicitly adopted in Berg's (1968) book on Risinghill, a London comprehensive school opened in 1960 but closed in 1965. The school was noted in educational circles for its far-reaching changes in teacher–pupil relationships, largely inspired by the headmaster, with some staff attempting to develop more expressive relationships with the pupils. The arguments used at the time of the closure of the school were that the arrangements at the school and its administration had lost the confidence of the parents. The authorities claimed that the school was closed because a majority of Islington parents did not want to send their children there. In 1964 only 76 parents made Risinghill the first choice for their eleven-year-olds, 29 named it as their second choice and the other 37 pupils admitted that year had failed to get places in the schools of their first and second choices. Ninety-eight out of its first 240 first-form places went unfilled.

Berg's book does not deal fully with the complexities of the situation. Her world, appears to be divided into those who supported the head and those who did not. There is no clear examination of the views of the staff and the parents and no consideration of the problems of leadership in a new school where a head has new ideas he wishes the staff to try out. Instead we are faced with a picture of administrators who wanted 'someone who would keep a school quiet and orderly, a man who would only have to stroll through the playground and you could hear a pin drop; and the politicians who wanted someone who could be manipulated or who at least would show he was grateful to be chosen'. The teachers were characterized as being in two main groups; first, the child-centred ones who supported the head and 'were the mature human beings . . . they could walk alongside the children . . . they knew . . . that they simply have to be helped to grow by people who have faith and delight in their growing'. The teachers who were not happy under the head's leadership 'had long ago surrendered their personality, the wishes and beliefs of their personal life . . . They told themselves that children should be quiet, that

60

they should be afraid of you, that you should be able to hear a pin drop when you crossed the playground, that children were naturally bad and needed the badness beaten out of them, that individuality must be crushed down by will-power and that there was satisfaction in this, and that God would reward people who kept their desks tidy, their lines straight, and never splashed outside the lavatory bowl' (Berg, 1968, p. 63).

Clearly such studies add little to an understanding of the complexities of the change process and the need at the moment is for more case studies which present us with a coherent picture of the process of educational change. Ideally we could hope for studies of similar innovations introduced into a number of organizations varying in one or more organizational characteristics, for example, the average age of the staff, staff experience, degree of staff autonomy, leadership style of the head-teacher or the relationship between the wider environment and the organization, or for innovations of varying degree of complexity introduced into organizations with similar organizational characteristics.

At present nothing of this scale has been attempted and the most ambitious attempt to undertake a series of studies concerned with change is that produced by research workers at the request of the Centre for Educational Research and Innovation (CERI) and reported in *Case Studies of Educational Innovation* (1973). The problems of this group of studies are clear from an examination of the studies of innovation at the school level. The schools were selected because they were seen to be experimental and had come to be regarded as 'leading innovative educational establishments . . . who had been continuously able to improve their own practice'. How this was evaluated by CERI, (one school had only been open four months when the researcher arrived), and how the final selection of schools from England, Norway, Canada, Denmark and Finland was arrived at is unclear. The schools studied range from the Experimental Gymnas in Oslo set up as a result of the campaign by dissatisfied high school students protesting against the traditional approaches, content and methods of the academic school, the authoritarian system, the control they felt from teachers, from the examination system and from the role set of teachers and students, to a private school in Finland, drawing students from an upper middle-class background, where the innovations were mainly in the area of the curriculum. A further problem with these studies is that they are self-confessedly little more than impressionistic. Most of the studies relied on a series of in-depth interviews, mainly with the school administration, questionnaires, usually to the school staff, existing research reports and records, and the researchers' own perceptions and informal discussions at the school. The reports were completed at very different times in the schools' histories and how this affected the data presented is unclear. There is the suggestion in one investigation that the collection of data was taking place at a point of high stress for the school and that this affected the participants' recall of past events.

## Case studies of open education in the United States

A more interesting group are a number of case studies, independently undertaken, of attempts to implement 'open education' in the elementary schools in the United States in the 1960s. These researches were carried out separately, yet when viewed together they raise many of the important questions about innovation as well as exhibiting a variety of different approaches to the study of innovation.

### The research problem

Case studies of educational innovation raise especial problems for the relationship between the researcher and the researched. The researcher has to obtain permission and funds for his study and the groups involved in the promoting of change are likely to control access to the organization for the researcher. The fieldworker is dependent on developing a high level of trust with the people that he is studying and yet at the same time reaching a shared sense of the importance of realistic descriptions of efforts at educational change. Given the enthusiasm of promoting groups the researcher's attempt to describe the actualities of the change process might run into difficulties, 'the boss, after all, has the power to throw the researcher out, too!' (Lightall, 1973, p. 276). It has been suggested that the way out of this difficulty is that the data collected should be vigorously fed back and discussed with *all* classes of informants. Unfortunately this suggestion often appears to be diluted until the data are discussed, if at all, with the groups involved in the promoting of change.

In the case studies mentioned above a variety of different styles can be seen reflecting the renewed attention being paid to field-work and case studies in social science (Glaser and Strauss, 1967). In recent years attempts have been made to treat qualitative data in a more rigorous and systematic way as opposed to the lengthy and detailed descriptions which had previously resulted in very small amounts of theory. This has resulted in a systematization of the ways of collecting, assembling and presenting qualitative materials.

Gross, Giacquinta and Bernstein in *Implementing Organizational Innovations: A Sociological Analysis of Planned Educational Change* (1971) report on a study which relied on a relatively traditional use of the case study method. From an analysis of the available literature the authors came to the conclusion that existing formulations of the problem of implementing organizational innovations were too simplistic in their concentration on overcoming organizational members' *initial* resistance to change. Before entry into the school, therefore, the authors specified the essential objectives of the study and decided to undertake an intensive field study of an elementary school whose staff could be anticipated to hold positive attitudes to educational change. The school chosen to fit this requirement, Cambire School, containing nearly 200 pupils and eleven full-time teachers, was located in a lower-class urban area of the central city of an eastern metropolitan area of the United States. Nearly 60 per cent of the residents of this area were black and they had encountered serious financial, housing, transportation and educational problems. An extensive body of data was collected on the basis of field observations conducted over nearly a seven-month period, the examination of public and private documents, informal and formal interviews with the teachers, their administrators and other school personnel and through the administration of a personality test.

In contrast to this the increasingly sophisticated discussion of methodology (see Delamont, 1976) can be seen in the development of the 'ethnographic' or 'descriptive' use of the case study represented by the work of Waller (1965), Jackson (1968) and Henry

(1966). In the case studies of American elementary schools undergoing change this approach is represented most clearly by Smith and Keith's *Anatomy of Educational Innovation: An Organizational Analysis of an Elementary School* (1971). The study observed the attempt to implement a broad programme of the 'new elementary education' – team teaching, individualized instruction and multi-age groups – in a newly opened purpose-built elementary school, Kensington School, in a middle-class suburban school district in the USA. The investigation was seen by the researchers as a model-building study with the principal method of data collection being participant observation. This was supplemented by the almost simultaneous collection of data by informal interviews, intensive analysis of records, and verbatim accounts of meetings. The level of involvement of the researchers in the school was high; for example, during the study the school was in session for 177 days from September to June and the observers have field notes from 153 different days at the school or in the district. The research was seen to have two outcomes: first, the careful and accurate description of the events that make up the beginning of an innovative school and, second, the discussion of the events in a more general theoretical language which would have applicability beyond the particular case of the elementary school under study. The authors build models that hopefully explain their data and offer these as fruitful starting-points for verificational research. The advantage of such an approach is that it retains considerable flexibility, allowing the researcher to move from one hypothesis to another throughout the period of the research. The consequence of this freedom of movement and the exploratory nature of the case study is that such an approach can make few claims for widespread generalization.

Besides the major studies of the attempts at Kensington and Cambire schools to introduce the new elementary education, there is Myers's study of 'The opening of an open school' (1973) and Barth's *Open Education and the American School* (1972). The Myers study, though not as ambitious as the first two, is interesting because the school was opened largely as a result of pressures exerted by a group of parents on the district's board of education, and the 'institutional plan' (the objectives of the school and how they were to be carried out) was the responsibility of the teachers.

64

Barth's study describes the attempt by a mainly white teaching staff to implement open education in an elementary school with a largely Negro catchment area in an eastern USA city. The study differs from the others looked at because Barth was a participant in the school, the principal, and this represents an insider's view of an attempt to introduce open schooling.

*Theoretical implications*

In the discussion of the theories of planned change it was noted that in their attempts to account for the success or failure of planned organizational change, social scientists have generally tended to conceptualize the problem as one of overcoming organizational members' initial resistance to change. In the case of schools the organizational members are taken to be the teachers. As a consequence of this definition of the problem, many efforts to account for the success or failure of attempts to implement organizational change have focused on the ability of management or a change agent to overcome members' initial resistance to change. However, in many change situations, involving both the creation of new and the alteration of old settings, the staff hold, prior to the introduction of the innovation, a favourable orientation to change. In all the studies under consideration the staff were already in favour of change.

## Cambire School

The Cambire School study emphasizes the existence of a normative climate within the school that encouraged basic changes in educational programmes and practices. The researchers state that prior to the introduction of the innovation into the school all the teachers were trying out new curriculum materials in their classrooms or were experimenting with new teaching methods. Each was attempting to conform to a normative climate that stressed the need for schools to institute basic changes in their educational programmes and practices. Eight of the eleven teachers at the school were new that academic year and had been selected because they had expressed strong interest in educational change. Some had been recommended by their former principals as teachers who

65

were especially creative or interested in educational innovations. The innovation, a new definition of the teacher's role called the catalytic role medal, was described by its originator to the teachers in an official document in November 1966 as follows:

1 Teachers were expected to behave in ways that would assist children to learn according to their interests rather than in terms of a prescribed curriculum;
2 Teachers were expected to emphasize the process, not the content, of learning, and to allow pupils maximum freedom in choosing their own activities;
3 Teachers were expected to see that the classroom was saturated with a variety of educational materials, primarily self-instructional in nature, so that children could pursue their own interests;
4 Teachers were expected to act as facilitators of learning between children and materials and to encourage teaching of children by other children;
5 Teachers were expected to allow pupils to decide the materials they wished to work with, how long they would work with them, and with whom they wished to relate;
6 Teachers were expected to give pupils primary responsibility for directing their own learning and to assist them only when they perceived that their help was desired or needed.

(Gross *et al.*, 1970, p. 694)

Despite the support the researchers claim existed for the innovation when it was introduced to the teachers, six months later the researchers found hardly any effort being made to implement the innovation. The staff were devoting most of their time within the classroom to behaviour that tended to conform to the traditional role model of teaching and were giving minimal time to efforts to implement the catalytic role model. When the teachers were making efforts to implement the innovation, they generally did little more than allow their pupils to do what they wanted to do, short of physically harming each other, or directed the children in multi-activities. The researcher assess that 'the overall quality of innovative effort . . . consisted primarily of the teacher's insertion into traditionally scheduled, self-contained classrooms of varying "chunks" of free time for their pupils each week' (Gross *et al.*,

1971, p. 119). The conclusion of the study is that, despite the teachers being positively disposed to accept major organizational changes in the school when the innovation was presented to them, this was a case of a failure to implement a major innovation. The authors suggest that one must search for alternative conceptualizations of the problem and they place particular emphasis on the unresolved problems or barriers to which staff may be exposed as they attempt to implement an innovation.

Gross *et al.* (1971, pp. 196–7) stress the existence or development of five major barriers during the period of attempted implementation of the catalytic role model. They stress that the clarity of an innovation to organizational members needs to be taken into account in conceptual schemes designed to explain the success or failure of implementation efforts. In the Cambire study observations of the teachers suggested that most of them did not have a clear image of the role performance expected of them. As one teacher put it 'I still really don't have a clear understanding of the innovation, and I can assure you that I'm not the only one'. Though the innovation is described by the researchers as 'a promising educational innovation' and as 'a major innovation' it appears to have remained mainly inside the Director's head and even there to have been remarkably unclear. The crucial importance of clarity about the new role model required by an innovation is underlined by Sarason who points out 'that if this question remains unanswered or remains in the realm of boring platitudes or unanalysable abstractions we stand a good chance of demonstrating that for the child, the more things change, the more they remain the same' (Sarason, 1971, p. 111). The Cambire study indicated the further problems created by the staff lacking the skills and knowledge required to perform the new role and the necessary materials and equipment.

Another obstacle pointed to was the existence of organizational arrangements that were incompatible with the catalytic role model. At Cambire, at the time of the announcement of the new role model, three practices existed which were incongruent with the new role model and, therefore, required alteration: the rigid scheduling of school time, the assignment of pupils to classrooms according to age, and the use of subject-oriented record cards. Two of the three organizational arrangements were never altered during the period of implementation and the third, although adjusted to some extent, was still restrictive to a considerable degree. The final barrier was the development, during the period of attempted implementation, of staff resistance to making efforts to introduce the innovation. The staff were no longer willing to devote time and effort to trying to implement the innovation.

In their discussion of the study Gross *et al.* suggested that, because of prior formulations, studies so far available have concentrated their attention on the changes required of the teachers but have given little thought to the changes required of administration. At Cambire, during the period of time between announcement and assessment of the innovation, the administrators' leadership was minimal. The administration failed to recognize or to resolve the problems to which it exposed teachers when it asked them to implement the innovation. Believing that teachers should be autonomous professionals, the management failed to conceive of teachers as organizational members who must rely on their superiors to help them with many of their problems when they make efforts to implement innovations.

Gross *et al.* have usefully pointed to the undue emphasis placed on the organizational members' initial resistance to change as an explanation of the failure of innovation efforts. They have stressed the importance of viewing the implementation of organizational innovations not as an event but as a process that involves an interrelated set of conditions that can shift over time – for example, the acceptance or clarity of a change proposal. However, at times their initial formulation of the problem and their deliberate selection of a situation where organizational members were initially in favour of change appears to hinder the analysis. Under the influence of studies of innovation in industrial organizations, Gross *et al.* have a tendency to treat innovation in education as a product to be introduced into the school. The value conflicts which surround the idea of educational change, even when the staff are in favour of change, are treated superficially.

At the Cambire School, despite the teachers' enthusiasm and even eagerness for educational change, they revealed mixed reactions on the announcement of the innovation by their superiors. Nine out of the ten teachers reported that they agreed with the objectives of the innovation. As one staff member put it 'I don't think you can disagree with the objective that we want to make thinkers out of the kids. We want to make them enjoy school, we want to make them intellectually more powerful, we want to give them a better self-image. I would say I definitely agree with his goals' (Gross *et al.*, 1971, p. 143). However, of the ten teachers interviewed with regard to their initial impressions of the innovation three of the teachers had general reactions that could be classed as positive, three as essentially ambivalent and four as somewhat negative. Thus only three of the ten teachers studied who were going to implement the innovation were wholeheartedly in support of it at the outset.

The apparent readiness of the teachers to make efforts to implement the innovation after it was presented to them in November came as a surprise to the administrators. Though the teachers were receptive to educational change, it is important to note that the role performance of these teachers was still fundamentally traditional in nature. The basic objective of teacher performance, prior to the announcement of the innovation, was typical of that in most schools classifiable as traditional, that is, the imparting of a particular body of knowledge and a set of skills to groups of children during regular periods each day. Despite the fact that the teachers were in favour of change the authors comment that 'the innovation was based on a set of assumptions about the nature of the child and the learning process different from those held by most of the teachers' (Gross *et al.*, 1971, p. 167). The problem raised by these basic differences is underemphasized and the suggestion is made of a complete programme of teacher re-training so that the teachers could obtain new skills as well as a set of new educational attitudes and values and a new way of viewing the phenomenon of schooling.

In the Cambire study there are clear indications of the drawbacks of resting a mode of enquiry on a prior set of assumptions and a related theory and methodology. Such dependence upon narrowly conceived lines of study can lead to narrow sets of conclusions. For example, Gross *et al.*'s assumption that staff generally in favour of educational change are also likely to be less resistant to any one particular educational change needs to be empirically tested in educational settings. Staff who are generally in favour of educational change are likely to be committed to particular types of educational change and thus may be even more resistant to change which they see as being in an undesired direction. There is no discussion in the Cambire study of why three of the four teachers who maintained that the innovation would not work anticipated no positive consequences for pupils and why all four teachers saw negative consequences for the pupils as a result of the innovation. These statements must be set against the researchers' note that 'all the teachers, even those who were classified as "negative", reported a willingness in November to make efforts to try to implement the innovation' (Gross *et al.*, 1971, p. 145).

The difficulties of attempting to implement change with a staff who are predisposed to change are well illustrated in Barth's case study. He notes that 'somehow, in the course of being interviewed and hired, each was led to believe not only that he would have an important place in the new programme but that *his* values, *his* orientation, and *his* strategies for change were uniquely valuable and appropriate for this inner-city situation. Each was led to believe that he had been singled out for inclusion in the programme *because* he believed what he did and *because* his values were consonant with the broader plans of the programme' (Barth, 1972, p. 125). This led to the school obtaining academically high powered staff who represented different, often mutually exclusive, assumptions about children, learning and knowledge and diverse techniques for solving the problems of inner-city schools. The dangers of this approach to implementation of educational innovation are clearly pointed to by Barth: 'You cannot hire able, bright, energetic idealistic people who, at the same time, have no convictions and can be programmed like marionettes in some ideological or pedagogical direction at the command of an authority' (Barth, 1972, p. 172).

## Kensington School

The most detailed study available of attempts to implement 'open' education in the USA is Smith and Keith's study of Kensington School. Kensington was intended to be revolutionary in three respects: it had a new open-plan building which won national architectural awards; a new staff, brought together to teach in teams, employing the catalytic role model; and a completely individualized learning system for the pupils, who were to be unstreamed, ungraded and encouraged to be independent. The study is explicitly concerned with the problems created in the implementation of educational ideas new not only to the individual school but also to the educational system. For the staff of the school ideas were their referents rather than schools already in question; doctrine and published sources were sought as arbitrators of issues.

At Kensington the administrators of the district were well aware of the literature which noted that resistance to change among staff can affect the process of implementation. They did not want old solutions to educational problems and believed that it would be easier to train inexperienced personnel in new approaches rather than to retrain experienced personnel whether or not they were initially oriented towards change. Consequently the staff selected for Kensington were chosen for their minimal prior commitments and were therefore unusual and in some ways unique. They were intellectually able, cosmopolitan rather than local, relatively inexperienced at teaching and with a general liberal democratic political orientation. Besides obtaining initial congruence with the formal doctrine of the school by selection of staff, the administrators also set up, prior to the opening of the school, a month's workshop for the staff including training groups and regular contacts with consultants and the researchers. Consequently the level of commitment of the staff was much higher than in the Cambire study: 'almost everyone had made a testimonial of some kind of extreme faith in the new school and what it is trying to do' (Smith and Keith, 1971, p. 90). The T-group experience which was organized as part of the four-week workshop for all staff provided opportunities for expressions of faith, though the public testimonial statements also fostered an over-exaltation of the virtues of Kensington.

Yet, despite this extremely favourable context for innovation there was an early retreat from progressive to traditional methods. In some of the divisions there was an early switch away from 'total teams' to working within an almost totally self-contained structure. Immediately after the first year of the innovation the superintendent of the school took a leave of absence for a year and then resigned. The curriculum director left after the first year to take a job with a charitable foundation and the principal left in the middle of the second year. Only eight of the original twenty-three teaching staff returned for the second year and only two of the original group returned for a third. Almost all the teachers who came for the second year departed before the third. 'New faculty were more traditional, and Kensington as both dream and reality was gone' (Smith and Keith, 1971, p. 17).

In analysing their data Smith and Keith draw heavily on a functionalist perspective emphasizing the interdependency of parts of the system as well as utilizing the concept of manifest and latent functions and dysfunctions. They use the term *formal doctrine* to apply to the point of view or perspective about themselves, their problems, and their environment that all groups and organizations develop. In highly innovative schools such as Kensington the formal doctrine represents 'the complex combination of a view that is visionary, that is highly conscious and that is highly codified'. Important aspects of the formal doctrine at Kensington were the notions of 'wrongs-to-be-righted' – the wrongs and 'evils' of traditional education that Kensington was to alter and replace – and the total commitment from the staff which would be required to bring about such changes. The formal doctrine, it is suggested, has the manifest function of providing a guide for action as well as serving to buoy up spirits when reality flagged. It is suggested, however, that a well codified and abstract formal doctrine has dysfunctional consequences in masking organizational realities and allowing for self-deception. The authors further differentiate between the *mandate*, the formal charge or directive given by the legitimate authority, the superintendent and indirectly by the school board and the community, and the *Institutional Plan* which is the particular conception of the doctrine developed by the principal, in this case prior to the workshop. Finally, one can speak of the individual staff member's conceptions or *schemas*. Each staff member held his own view or schema of Kensington seemingly generated out of personal needs and goals, early conversations about the school and early documents. Differences as to teaching methods, materials, pupil control and staff organization were prevalent. The staff was verbal and articulate in isolating and elaborating 'reasonable but incompatible' individual interpretations of what Kensington stood for. An inability to merge these individual schemas into a common enough framework, an agreed interpretation of the doctrine, was one of the causes of the later splits in the teams.

In an interesting analysis the authors point to the problems created by a strong Institutional Plan, individual staff schemas and 'democratic administration'. The observer records 'I keep getting a very strong image of Eugene [the principal] as someone who wants to be a democratically oriented school administrator, and, yet, who has an ego-involved idea that he sees as more real and more ideal than anything else that might be arrived at. In that sense he seems to be a man with more faith in his own ideas . . . than in the possibility of this group of people arriving at a better Institutional Plan' (Smith and Keith, 1971, p. 31). Though committed to 'democratic' administration Kensington struggled with problems related to democratic administration, authority and the locus of decision-making. At different times it appeared that decisions were on a 'participant determining' (consensus) basis, on an implicitly parliamentarian (voting) basis and on a democratic centralism basis (the principal as final authority). The emphasis placed, at times, on staff members determining policy led to the development of considerable frustration when staff suggestions that ran counter to the plan were never put into operation.

In the study the authors make a further useful distinction between the formal doctrine and the *façade* – the formal doctrine as it was presented to the public. For an innovative school the 'public' is clearly multiple, including the parents who are the immediate patrons of the school, the residents of the school district, the broader audience and also the national community. The study analyses how the media attended selectively to the most favourable aspects of school activities and how the principal encouraged the dissemination of only positive information to the parents resulting in a discrepancy between the organizational face presented to the public and the reality of the school.

*Resistance to change*

Another fertile source of ideas for the interpretation of their data came from the field of the sociology of social movements. As

73

noted before, the ideas to be implemented in this school were new to the educational system. In their discussion of the staff of the school the authors are influenced by Hoffer's (1952) work on the true believer. In his book concerned with the active revivalist phase of mass movements Hoffer notes that this phase is dominated by the true believer – the man of fanatical faith who is ready to sacrifice his life for a holy cause. Such true believers, with their extremes of enthusiasm and excitement, are probably needed for the realization of vast and rapid change. It is only later when a mass movement has passed its vigorous stage that it begins to attract people who are interested in their individual careers. The Kensington study is replete with religious imagery showing how the staff had a belief system which saw the school as playing an important part in the quest, the crusade, the vision, the search for the grail. All of this clearly implies a staff whose values and behaviour contrast sharply with those characteristic of the 'typical' members of school staffs.

The importance of this aspect of the study can be seen if we examine again the notion of resistance to change. Existing patterns are not readily given up and are likely to be particularly resistant to change where there is strong motivational, personal and social support. The Kensington study illustrates how, for true believers, from the formal doctrine and the façade comes the motivation to carry on beyond what real, day-to-day results seem to justify. It is the doctrine and façade that provide reassurance for the true believer in the face of no demonstrable evidence for success and even in the presence of failure. For the true believer 'responses of opposition and apathy from one's public may be viewed as reinforcement for the mission . . . failure conceived as opposition or lack of support from one's public and constituents is unknown, it only serves to legitimate the tasks of evangelism' (Smith and Keith, 1971, p. 116). Myers similarly notes that because of their belief in the doctrine of the school, most of the teachers maintained a positive attitude despite the growing opposition to their educational programme from the parents and the administration. It is this 'true belief' which Smith and Keith claim will allow the staff to speak of 'next year' and seek further opportunities to continue their mission.

Unfortunately a major omission of the Kensington study is

any detailed data on the staff leaving the project, their aspirations and plans for the future. While the opening of the school is chronicled in great detail, the later stages are treated, at times, sketchily. However, the contrast between the staff reactions to the failures of the innovations at Cambire and Kensington is instructive as regards long-term commitment. In the Cambire study resentment was quickly turned against the director. The staff saw the innovation as the 'property' of the director and felt he was using them in an unprofessional manner to promote 'his' innovation. At Kensington despite the lack of unity at times, the principal's farewell party saw the staff united for 'as the people joked, the spirit was much more of we against them – the forces outside in the community which were trying to stifle the school and trying to attack the principal. I had the feeling . . . that the villain in the eyes of the teachers this year was the district, which wouldn't support the basic idea that the school was trying to convey' (Smith and Keith, 1971, p. 5).

## The alternative of grandeur

Examination of these case studies shows that they all followed the strategy of innovation designated by Smith and Keith as the 'alternative of grandeur'. They adopted a revolutionary strategy towards change which involved simultaneous change in persons, interactions, programmes and structures. Their attempts to implement pervasive changes involved a high-risk strategy with potentially large rewards. This strategy of change can be contrasted with the strategy of gradualism outlined by Etzioni in his essay 'A gradualist strategy at work' (Etzioni, 1966). The gradualist strategy, implying the alteration of a few components at a time, involves lower levels of uncertainty and fewer unintended consequences, decreased time pressure, an increased interval for major change, limited decisions related to the changes and decreased demand on resources. Proponents of this strategy claim that by amplifying the close and underplaying the remote this will lead to an increased likelihood of success in initial goals and that for both the organization and its staff this reinforces activities, increases esteem and leads to further changes. Smith and Keith suggest that the choice of the alternative of grandeur strategy must be placed into a wider context. The school district had a history of political conflict over a prior superintendent who was fired, rehired and later was given a position as a district-wide consultant. Many of the changes sought by the superintendent, the curriculum director and the principal were not congruent with the lower middle-class values of the community. The leaders were cosmopolitans rather than locals; their basic commitments were to the field of education instead of the school district; consequently time was short. Their choice must also be viewed against a contemporary pronouncement from the US Office of Education stating that 'The program of each Experimental School must be implemented in the first year of operation rather than in stages over the 5 years' (Smith and Keith, 1971, p. vi). From their analysis Smith and Keith suggest that the concepts of unanticipated consequences, unintended outcomes and the magnitude of resources are vital to anyone contemplating change. A more pervasive change is accompanied by more unanticipated events. 'The more outcomes that are unanticipated, the greater becomes the need for additional resources both to implement the program and to respond to the increased variety introduced by the unintended events' (Smith and Keith, 1971, pp. 367–8).

A fundamental limitation of this group of studies is that they are still firmly set within the tradition of the management of innovation. It will be argued in the next chapter that the focus on the relationship between administrators and teachers was at the expense of a detailed look at the other participants or even at the interaction between the participants in the change process. It is worth noting that a further limitation of these studies is a lack of systematic data on what teachers were doing. For example, in the Cambire study it was only after the interviews were completed, in late April, that the researchers began to study intensively what was taking place in the classroom, and then they only observed over three weeks. In the Cambire and the Kensington studies the teachers did not implement the innovation in the heads of the administrators but what changes, if any, in their teaching behaviour were evident?

While the studies point to the 'failure' of the innovation, what in fact had failed to be implemented were the plans of the Superintendents and principals. This is the only sense in which the inno-

76

vations can be considered 'failures'. In the interviews with the administrators it became clear that the ideas for these new role models for teachers came from a variety of sources, but mainly from Leicestershire. The studies suggest that the ideas did not come from observation of the practice of teachers in Leicestershire but from reading the popularized accounts which purported to show what was going on there in the classrooms. The similarity between the descriptions of teachers' behaviour in the classroom at the end of the year in Cambire and Boydell's (1971) and Berlak *et al.*'s (1975) description of teacher behaviour in Leicestershire classrooms is striking. In the Cambire study, as previously noted, it was claimed that the overall quality of innovative effort revealed that it consisted primarily of the teachers' insertion into traditionally scheduled, self-contained classrooms of varying 'chunks' of free time for their pupils each week. This can be compared with Berlak's description of Mrs Lawton's classroom in a Leicestershire school. What we lack from the American studies are data which shows what changes, if any, in teacher behaviour took place during the period the schools were studied and how the teachers viewed such changes.

The judgment of the innovation in 'success–failure' terms with the evaluation made simply in terms of whether the teacher behaviour is consistent with the ideas or principles contained in the administrator's institutional plan can easily lead to an obscuring of the processes of change that have occurred subsequent to the introduction of the innovation. The importance of viewing this process in terms other than 'success–failure' is well illustrated in Bernbaum's (1973) study of Countesthorpe College, which deliberately avoids making such evaluations. He does point, however, to the nature of the staff dissatisfactions with the innovations at the college.

Bernbaum's study was undertaken at a time when the college had only been open for four months and the construction work on the site had not been completed. Furthermore, while the school was planned as an upper school for 1,400 14–18 year olds and as a community college, at this stage it only had pupils of 11–14 years. At this early stage over half of the teachers were not satisfied with the operation of individualized learning at the school. The sources of their dissatisfaction fell into two categories: doubts about the ability and opportunity of the teachers to prepare adequate material and doubts about the effectiveness of the material prepared, particularly in its usefulness to motivate all the children. The existence of anxiety over the problems of motivation in a system of individualized learning was further suggested when the teachers were offered nine items from which to choose those factors which might constrain them in the innovations they wished to adopt. Thirty per cent of the choices were for 'lack of adequate teaching material' and a further 25 per cent emphasized 'the previous educational experience of the children'. The remaining seven factors received only 45 per cent of the selections.

Similar levels of dissatisfaction existed among the staff with regard to the working of staff democracy in the school. While only 5 per cent of the teachers claimed to be 'very satisfied' with the operation of staff democracy, 45 per cent were positively 'not satisfied'. The sources of this dissatisfaction varied from teachers resenting the cumbersome and time-wasting machinery that is part of the democratic process to fears of the development of an oligarchy. The area of innovation which the staff rated as the most important – 'greater equality in social relations between staff and children' – had the highest level of satisfaction.

The school has now been in operation for five years and later reports point to some of the changes which have occurred (Makins, 1975). With regard to staff democracy it soon became clear that it was too unwieldy to have all decisions taken by a moot open to all, including non-teaching staff and students, and so it was decided to constitute four rotating standing committees to run the school. However, any decision of these standing committees can be challenged and a moot called. In the second year of the school the moots became increasingly concerned with failures on the academic and the pastoral side. The core curriculum/option system was seen as not working for a number of pupils at the school. A recent article noted that 'part of the trouble was undoubtedly that teachers have been over-ambitious and over-optimistic about how much they could lay on in terms of a fairly individualized curriculum options, in a brand new school which was innovating on all fronts' (Makins, 16.6.75, p. 17). In an attempt to overcome these problems a new system was introduced whereby incoming fourth-year students were divided into 'teams' manned by teachers mainly from the 'core' disciplines of English, Social Studies and Mathematics. The idea is that the team teachers get to know their students very well, both as people and as learners, in a way that a system of specialist teachers backed by pastoral staff makes almost impossible. Within the framework of Bernbaum's early discussion it can be seen that the changes introduced place even more emphasis on the nature of the relationship between the teacher and the pupil. From the perspective of the teachers in the school these changes are seen as developing from the original goals of the school and are claimed, not as a retreat to more conventional methods, but as a way of making the school more radical.

In this chapter it has been claimed that in the case studies so far undertaken, their implicit acceptance of the framework of the management of change has led to an emphasis on the relationships between administrators and teachers at the expense of other participants in the change process. In the following two chapters an attempt will be made to bring together material on two neglected groups in the change process – parents and students.

# 6

# Innovation
# and the community

In the last two chapters we have explored how the prevailing
framework of the management of innovation displays only limited consideration of many important issues. Crucial areas such
as the control of innovation, the power relationships between
teachers and their clients and the implications of innovations for
these relationships have been underexplored. Earlier community
studies such as the Lynds' classic studies of *Middletown* (1929)
and *Middletown in Transition* (1937), carried out in the USA in
the 1920s and 1930s, showed a keen awareness of these points.
They examined the conflicts arising from the introduction of
innovations in education and looked at the effect of these within
the framework of the local community and its politics.

According to one version of early American education, the
schools served to extend and transmit the values upon which
parents, teachers, religious and civic leaders were in substantial
agreement. However, the Lynds claim that during the twentieth
century Middletown's schools had gradually become an area of
conflict. As home, church and community became areas of con-
fused alternatives, so education itself developed 'a professional

point of view of its own, of the culture, but also somewhat over against the culture' (Lynd and Lynd, 1937, p. 226). They traced how a philosophy of education based on individual differences was diffused to Middletown as a formal 'philosophy of education' by remote philosophers in university graduate schools of education, and how this philosophy was 'no more consonant with certain dominant elements in Middletown at present than was the philosophy of Socrates with that of the Athens of his day' (Lynd and Lynd, 1937, p. 226). This 'education for individual differences' introduced sharp conflicts into the community particularly as at this time the local culture appeared to be putting renewed stress on elements making for solidarity and unanimity. The Lynds predicted that when Middletown confronted a period of high taxes and a depressed standard of living, the community, in turn, would try to exert more control over the philosophy of its schools.

The Lynds' point was taken up again by Charter when he challenged the view that 'the American public school system supports the values of the dominant social class of their constituent communities' (Charters, 1953, p. 268). He suggested that this view, based on evidence showing that teachers, school administrators and school board members had a middle-class bias, and that community values were pervasive, ignored the growth of professionalism and bureaucracy in public education.

The essentially dynamic nature of the power relationships between teachers and the community is suggested in the Lynds' studies and the events of the last decade in the USA have shown how, once the question of political concerns in school decisions is raised, and hence the possibility of more compromise, the autonomy of the professional educator is diminished. In recent years critics have been alleging that schools, and the teachers in them, have become too insulated from criticism and must be forced to become more responsive and accountable to the community. In the USA poor achievement by urban youngsters has been viewed by an increasing number of parents, whether correctly or not, as evidence that the professional bureaucracy has not been taking its responsibilities seriously. The notion that the responsibility for determining what goes on in the school should lie solely with the teachers is being challenged. Defenders of parents' rights have loudly asserted their claims that 'parents typically educate' and in their contention 'they are the only ones who have a clear-cut right to educate' (Bereiter, 1973). Attempts have been made to separate out the expert and non-expert tasks in education, for example, Litwak and Meyer claim that 'the setting of basic educational goals is perhaps the clearest instance of a task where the knowledge of the professional educator may be less effective than that of the citizen parent . . . [these tasks do] require some technical judgment but they fundamentally involve value-judgments. Insofar as the educational system is expected to reflect community values, community members rather than professionals are usually better able to say what these values are' (Litwak and Meyer, 1974, p. 11).

In England and Wales, similar feelings have been evident in the 'Great Debate' of 1976 and 1977. Critics complained of declining standards in the schools and of secondary school curricula insufficiently matched to life in a modern industrial society, while others felt that schools gave insufficient attention to the wishes of parents and under-valued the contribution they could make to the education of their children. Weaver, a former civil servant at the Department of Education and Science, is reported as saying 'The public have called the bluff of the teaching profession and are demanding the right to say what ought to be the ends of education instead of leaving them to the mystique of the profession' (quoted in *The Times Educational Supplement*, 24 September 1976).

The new emphasis on the role parents can play has been formally recognized in a number of recent publications. The Green Paper, *Education in Schools: A Consultative Document* (Department of Education and Science, 1977a) recognizes parents should be given more information about the schools and should be consulted more widely. The Taylor Committee (DES, 1977b), set up to review the arrangements for the management and government of maintained primary and secondary schools in England and Wales, has recognized that people outside the formal educational system have an important contribution to make in the way their children are taught, and recommended, among other things, that the governing bodies of schools become the forum for consideration of the suitability of new educational ideas and methods for the school. One of the prime motivations behind the internal review of the committee and staffing structure of the Schools Council begun in 1976 has been concern over the dominance of the body by organized teachers' groups, particularly the National Union of Teachers. It was felt that the interests of the local education authorities, the Department of Education and Science as well as the wider community, had been set aside. At the same time there is a growing recognition (see DES, 1977a, p. 16) that if schools are to become more accountable to the communities which they serve, a coherent and soundly based means of assessment for the education system as a whole, for schools, and for individual pupils is required. The creation of the Assessment of Performance Unit is seen by some as a possible instrument to achieve this aim at the national level at least.

However, at the same time as some parents are seeking to enlarge their control of the schools some teachers and administrators in their search for professionalism are striving to increase their autonomy from lay control and teacher associations and unions, with their more militant tactics, are becoming an important part of the politics of education. In the USA Boyd (1976, p. 540) has pointed out how the administrators view themselves as far from dominating the local educational policy-making process but as struggling with a variety of interest groups and forces that not infrequently threaten to neutralize their ability to provide any kind of effective leadership. There have been clashes particularly in situations where teaching staff, largely white, feel they are losing their control over their own professional autonomy and over the teaching process to angry citizens sometimes not too well educated and largely black (Berube and Gittell, 1970). The impact of these recent demands for decentralization, community control and accessibility can be seen in Mann's (1976) recent study of school administrators (including school principals) and local democracy in the USA. He differentiates between three roles administrators take in relation to the community: the trustee – someone whose decisions are based on his own values, even though the represented may disagree; the delegate – someone who is guided by expressed citizen preference even at the expense of his own best judgment; and lastly the politico – someone who borrows from either trustee or delegate styles as dictated by situations but has some internally consistent rationale for doing so. Mann's study, based on interviews and case studies of 161 school administrators found, predictably, that the trustee style was most frequently adopted, but that 30 per cent did adopt a delegate style. These results are indicative of the impact of the movement to restore more power into the hands of the community at the expense of the professional.

## Teacher–community relationship in Britain

As Baron and Tropp (1961, p. 545) have pointed out, the area of teacher–community relationships has constantly attracted the attention of American sociologists of education because it was seen as a 'social problem' affecting the whole success of the educational enterprise. In Britain, however, the moves to 'insulate' gradually the schools and education from popular pressure at the local level have resulted in a more limited concern with this area. Musgrove and Taylor (1969) have claimed that over the last hundred years there has grown up in our midst a new despotism: the rule of the teachers. They assert that there has been a growing loss of parental power accelerated by the Education Act of 1902 which created local education authorities remote from parents and designed to act as a buffer between the school and the parents.

Where suggestions have been made for closer co-operation between teachers and parents (e.g. the Plowden Report, 1967, chapter 4) co-operation appears to mean persuading parents to accept the views of teachers without any encroachments on the staff's professional autonomy. The efforts to form Parent–Teachers' Associations in England have been essentially attempts to enlist parental support for the work of the school. An American observer of the English educational system, Fisher, discusses the organization of a Parent–Teachers' Association by a progressive primary school head whose school reflected many current 'advanced' practices and provided widespread freedom for the children. He notes how 'after the constitution had been adopted, he (the head) welcomed all the new members but warned them that if they started to interfere with his school, he would have no hesitation about dissolving the PTA forthwith' (Fisher, 1972, p. 24).

Consequently it is not surprising to discover that in this country administrators appear to adopt a trustee stance. Administrators accept that this role is justified because they feel that this is what the public would want if only they knew what the administrators know. Even proponents of change who see a future in which people will increasingly participate in making decisions about what goes on in their community appear to adopt this approach. Advocates of community schools, such as Midwinter, have argued 'For instance, if such a school with parents roaming at will, with nightly tenancies for local groups, and with local representation on school governmental boards – had dedicated itself to the narrow academic aim of improving the literacy and numeracy attainments of the select minority, then it would be failing sorrowfully to fulfil its "community" function' (Midwinter, 1973, pp. 10–11). The expertise which many innovators claim for themselves is well brought out in Duane's reply to criticism of Berg's book on Risinghill. He claims that 'there remains . . . a small minority of men and women with clarity of insight into the needs of democracy, with professional skills and with integrity . . . [who can] give their pupils some sense of personal worth, some feeling of real identity and the beginning of confidence in their own powers' (Duane, 1968, p. 135). Such educators have confidence in their own insights and believe that though these will cause anxieties in those who have different views, the hostility will be 'from those who emotionally reject change' (McMullen, 1972, p. 49).

How one identifies those who emotionally support or reject change is unclear, what is clear is that this point of view is connected with a position which sees the expert as having the right and duty to impose his view of the future and of the educational system on parents and children, willing or not. That what is seen by some groups as 'leadership' is likely to be seen by others as 'manipulation' is exemplified by Lightall's view of the 'failure' of Kensington School as a victory involving 'the clear cut routing of virtually all of those who had had a hand in the audacious attempt to impose the minority clique's reality upon the community and the larger school system – the majority – using the majority's funds to boot' (Lightall, 1973, p. 260). This strong sense of professional identity was again illustrated in the recent report on the William Tyndale school. The head and the majority of the teachers in the school had a strong definition of themselves as 'professionals'. The headmaster seemed to resent the fact that parents who were not 'professional teachers' took it upon themselves to criticize in any way the teaching methods that were being adopted at the school and felt that ultimately the teacher must decide how best to teach the children – regardless of the view of the parents (Auld, 1976, pp. 80 and 286).

This present-day situation of the teachers' authority *vis-à-vis* parents is rooted in the historical tradition of the teachers' intellectual separation from the majority of the parents. In particular the graduate teacher acquired the status of his subject – he became physicist, or historian, or chemist, and hence linked with all the scholars and scholarship associated with his specialism. Until the most recent times it could be assumed that the graduate would have been educated full time at a university, an institution which stands at the apex of the English educational system with standards that are internationally recognized. For non-graduates, particularly those concerned with young children, the educational knowledge gap between teachers and parents was narrower and hence one basis of their authority was largely absent. As suggested before, innovations have to be viewed in terms of their effects on the power relationships between teachers and their clients. Observers (Musgrove and Taylor, 1969; Bernstein, 1975; Sharp and Green, 1975) have suggested that the rapid growth and acceptance of 'progressive' educational ideas by primary school teachers may be associated with attempts on their part to generate a professional ideology and occupational structure which served to increase their autonomy and status. Teachers can present themselves as having certain forms of 'objective' psychological expertise on which they base their pedagogy. It is suggested that this expertise, with its attendant vocabulary of 'needs', 'readiness', 'interests', etc. leaving the mark of the 'expert' and the 'scientific researcher', plays an important part in increasing the autonomy of the teacher. Sharp and Green argue that it promotes in the parents a perception of the teachers as, in some sense, psychiatrists possessing the appropriate specialist knowledge. This view allows the teacher to preserve an area of very high discretion in the classroom in regard to general organization, atmosphere and discipline.

Rather than having a picture of parents as powerless, one should see that different parents have different degrees of power with reference to the school situation. Parents with adequate financial resources are free to buy a schooling for their children which more fully reflects their wishes but even within the state system parents have varying degrees of power and teachers and innovators are well aware of this. The relative powerlessness of many working-class parents can be gauged from the fact that many large-scale innovations involving major changes in the school environment have first been implemented in working-class areas and Bernbaum has suggested that 'There is a real possibility . . . that . . . the main focus for experiment and innovation in the long run may be the non-achieving working class' (Bernbaum, 1973, p. 20). The same point is made in the following passage written by an American observer of change in British infant school education. He claims that 'it is hardly an accident that the open classroom movement received its initial impetus in working-class, not, middle-class infant schools or that the movement was able to have clear effects in a society which sends only a very small proportion of its children to colleges' (Wallach, 1971, pp. 548–9).

Sharp and Green studied a school situated on a large new local authority housing estate. The inhabitants had previously lived in poor accommodation in various parts of the city and had either been allocated housing on this estate through slum-clearance schemes, or had been selected by virtue of their high priority on the council's lists. The headmaster of the school, a progressive primary school called 'Mapledene' by the authors, showed recognition of these parents lack of power when he said that 'working-class people, such as I deal with here, don't have the same aspirations and therefore to some extent I don't have the same pressures that I would have if I tried to do the same thing in a middle-class area' (Sharp and Green, 1975, p. 53). Parents who were hostile to the school and the teachers in fact admitted to a sense of powerlessness. This powerless revealed itself in a number of ways: in recognition that their geographical and economic position gave the parents no choice of school; a realization that the parents had no sanctions they could bring to bear whereas the teachers had, which might result in the child being 'done down'; a lack of institutionalized authority behind the parents to give legitimacy to their complaints; a feeling of being deprived of access to information which might assist them in their case against the school; a realization that if the parents and teachers are going to get on well, 'then it must be on the teachers' terms' (Sharp and

Green, 1975, p. 213). An interesting contrast highlighting how parents have different access to power to influence the school situation is presented in the report on the enquiry into the William Tyndale School (Auld, 1976). The school served an area that was changing from a predominantly working-class one into an area of much wider social mix. Young professional married couples with children were moving into what were run-down terraced houses, renovating them and beginning to participate in and make their mark upon the social life and amenities of the area. As a result of the school's situation in an inner-city area with a declining population and falling school rolls, parents were able to exert their 'right to choose' the school for their child. The report suggests that it was mainly the more able children and children with 'better home circumstances' who were transferred elsewhere or withdrawn from the junior school. A group of parents and governors, mainly from middle-class backgrounds, using their knowledge of the educational and political system, their position within the local Labour Party and their contacts with the media were able to mobilize opposition to the head and the teachers when they had no success in modifying the school's policies.

Other important factors in explaining variations in the amount of power parents possess are the parents' place of residence and the possibility of their mobility and the amount of political pressure they are able to exert on the authority to change their children's place of schooling. Many of the nationally known innovations in education in this country have taken place in the private sector of education. For example, as Musgrove and Taylor point out 'the morality of Summerhill's "progressive" position is firmly based in the free and informed choices of clients for a particular form of educational experience out of a wide range of alternatives available to them' (Musgrove and Taylor, 1969, p. 85). However, for most parents who send their children to state schools the freedom of choice is largely illusory. Although section 76 of the 1944 Education Act gives it to them quite specifically – 'pupils are to be educated in accordance with the wishes of their parents' – it does so only in 'so far as it is compatible with the provision of efficient instruction and training and the avoidance of unreasonable public expenditure'. In practice this means in some areas, e.g. rural and semi-urban areas, this freedom is only nominal and, the local authorities insist, has to remain so where there is only one school in a neighbourhood or where one favoured school would burst its walls without some form of zoning. In these situations, only parents who can 'buy' schooling, who can afford to move home or who can exert sufficient pressure on the authority to change their child's place of schooling have any choice of an alternative form of schooling.

Carlsson (1964) has suggested that one important feature of state schools, as opposed to private schools, is that there is no struggle for survival, as their clients are guaranteed. This 'domestication' is seen by him as a crucial factor in explaining the schools' unwillingness to innovate. Yet in systems, such as the Leicestershire one, dealing essentially with rural and semi-urban areas, the parents' very lack of freedom of choice, the schools' guarantee of a new set of 'clients' every year, is supportive of the innovation. In the inner-city areas, however, with a falling population and declining schools rolls, where parental choice has been allowed innovative schools appear to have faced more difficulties. The enquiry into the William Tyndale School and the controversy surrounding Risinghill raise questions about Carlsson's suggested relationship between innovation and the 'domestication' of schools. In both these situations, where the parents were given some 'choice', one of the major impetuses for an evaluation of what was occurring was the failure of the schools to maintain their clientele. The authorities' claim in the Risinghill situation was that the school was closed because a majority of the Islington parents did not want to send their children there. Interestingly, one of the strategies employed by the head and teachers at William Tyndale was to attempt to 'lock in' the children already there. They did this by asking, unsuccessfully, the members of the North London Teachers' Association in neighbouring schools to oppose admission to their schools of children from William Tyndale (Auld, 1976, p. 295).

## Parents' views of education

The relative powerlessness of the working class in respect to schooling must be seen in relation to studies which have explored the extent of similarity/dissimilarity between the views of parents from various social strata and the proponent of innovation. In the USA Sieber and Wilder (1967) in their study of 'Teaching styles: parental preferences and professional role definitions' found that mothers preferred a content-oriented style of teaching more than any other, while a majority of teachers saw themselves as discovery-oriented. Over two-thirds of the mothers expressed role preferences that were not in accord with the self-descriptions of their child's teacher, and mothers who believed that teachers were not teaching the way they would like them to teach were much more often dissatisfied with teachers. Large differences were found between mothers in communities with differing socio-economic compositions: working-class mothers had a higher preference for the control and content style of teaching, while middle-class mothers tended to share with teachers the preference for a discovery-oriented style. Sieber and Wilder clearly point to the difficulties that are likely to arise when innovative schemes, involving changes in teaching styles, are introduced into working-class areas where mothers have an especially high preference for control-oriented teaching styles. This can be seen in Barth's (1972) account of the Lincoln-Attucks school. The parents appear to have been in favour of the school at the beginning and some of the early problems arose because parents from all over the town had sent children to 'reside' with uncles, aunts and friends in the Program's neighbourhood. What became increasingly clear was that the parents' implicit mandate to members of the Program staff was to improve dramatically the children's education, in the narrowest sense, without significantly changing anything else. The parents' model of education resembled that of a military academy and parents expected, wanted and demanded clear evidence that each pupil was under the control of the teacher at all times. Because of their failure to see parental expectations within the context of the wider social structure, few innovators appear to understand why many working-class parents should define a 'good education' as being what the children in the middle-class suburbs receive.

In Britain similar results can be seen in Musgrove and Taylor's (1969, ch. 3) findings produced from a survey of parents' expectations of teachers. Parents of children in the last two years of junior schools were selected for investigation. Sharp contrasts were found in expectations between those parents living in a municipal housing estate and those in a well-to-do residential area. On the municipal housing estate parents tended to place more responsibility on the school for training the child's behaviour – in part, at least, because they felt that teachers were more effective than themselves. In the well-to-do residential areas parents placed more emphasis on the responsibility of the home and parents to guide behaviour. Parents from the housing estate wanted teachers to encourage more 'basic' behaviour such as cleanliness and obedience and behaviour which would support adult authority. Of the parents in this area who gave particulars of the attitudes, virtues and qualities of personality which they wished the school to develop in their children, 70 per cent were concerned about various forms of unruly or anti-social behaviour. Fifty-two per cent specified training in obedience, respect for elders or 'not to be cheeky' and 18 per cent specified honesty, 'steadiness', truthfulness, respectability or 'curbing of bad manners'. Twenty per cent expected the school to teach 'manners' which appeared to mean very largely, if not exclusively, respect for elders and acceptance of adult authority. In the middle-class areas there was not so much stress on training in obedience and respect for elders and more emphasis was laid on 'secondary' virtues such as diligence and punctuality.

Studies of parent–child relationships are supportive of Musgrove and Taylor's findings and indicate the possibility of locating these different expectations in the wider social structure. Kohn (1969), for example, has attempted in a number of studies, some international, to relate parent–child relationships to differences in the conditions of life, and particularly the occupational conditions of the father, in different social classes. He suggests that it is the greater degree of self-direction present in middle-class occupations which leads them to value self-direction in their children and so to encourage in their children such qualities as curiosity and self-control. Working-class parents, on the other hand, stress such qualities as honesty, obedience and neatness, because in their working lives what is required of them is that they should follow explicit rules laid down by someone in authority. While criticisms have been made of Kohn's studies (e.g. the extent of inter-class variation, the emphasis on father's occupation) they are important in showing that parents' views of education cannot be viewed simply as irrational but must be seen as firmly embedded in their experiences within the wider society and as such not easily changed by an institution like the school.

Given these concerns it is surprising to find that few students of innovation have intensively interacted with parents in a variety of social situations or utilized them as key informants, informally or through structured interviews. Of the studies examined in the last chapter, the researchers rarely mention the parents of children at the Cambire school and in the Kensington study the data on parents were too limited to suggest very intensive analyses and generalizations. The most detailed, as well as the most provocative, study of parents and innovation is contained in Sharp and Green's study of 'Mapledene' School (particularly ch. 10). While they did not trace the development of parent perspectives over time or observe many samples of parent–parent, parent–pupil or parent–teacher interaction they did interview each parent once using an informal unstructured methodology. The researchers point to a high level of parental interest in education but an interest relating to the parental value conceptions of what they think education ought to be doing as well as to their definitions of what schools and educational systems actually are doing. In a similar way to other studies they show how, almost without exception, the parents attached great importance to their children learning to read, write and develop numeracy, and that this was an area of potential disagreement between the teachers and the parents. In their analysis Sharp and Green note how to the teacher a good parent is one who appears to defer to the teacher's superior knowledge, expertise and competence. However, the research showed that those children whom the teachers defined as good or bright pupils at school, and hence by the teachers' definition possessed of 'good parents', did in fact have parents who took upon themselves the role of the teacher at home, often in defiance of what they knew to be the teachers' disapproval of parents' interference. Nevertheless, at the same time as they were, in fact, interfering they had to manage the nature and extent of their involvement in order for it not to appear that trust had been taken away from the teacher. As Sharp and Green say, it is ironical that whilst the teachers think that they are engaged in compensatory education providing a wide variety of experiences for deprived children to work through their needs and become ready to learn, the differential readiness to learn is related to the extent to which parents have engaged in compensatory education to compensate for the deprivation in learning experiences that they feel their children have suffered at school [and that] those parents who are most in favour at the school are usually those who, amongst other things, appear by their actions in consistently teaching children to read etc. most critical of it. (Sharp and Green, 1975, p. 208)

As a corollary to this the unsuccessful parent may be one who fully embraces the role of the good parent, i.e. one who accepts that it is the teacher's responsibility and duty to teach the child without interference from the parent, or one who is not prepared to take the role of the good parent but rather communicates to the teacher his dissatisfaction with her competence and her failure to produce results. The authors suggest that this latter group may be defined by the school staff as disturbed or unstable, in a similar way perhaps to those who were seen by McMullen as 'emotionally rejecting change'. It must be stressed that this research is exploratory and although there is at times a certainty about the presentation of the conclusions the reader requires more adequate knowledge of the findings from which the conclusions were drawn.

The importance of parents' value conceptions of what they think education ought to be doing is shown again in the studies of large-scale innovation in the secondary school. These suggest that many parents do not necessarily object to educational innovations if these do not change the function of the school. For many parents, secondary schools function as selection agencies giving their children at least the chance of a good status in life. In the CERI studies, even in the school with the most subject-oriented innovations (Tapiola, Finland) Virtanen reports that '. . . the staff objective of extensive freedom of choice by the pupils aroused the parents' hostility. Such choice was believed not to be in the best interests of the children, who, the parents argued, need planned guidance. Also, the parents pointed out that it was good for the children to learn to perform difficult and unpleasant tasks' (Virtanen, 1973, p. 305). Bernbaum's study, in the early days of Countesthorpe, noted that reactions from parents favoured more conventional teaching, which they felt was easier to control and where results were more easily identified. He suggested that parental anxieties that the school might not meet their expectations with regard to instruction in subjects and social advancement were likely to continue unless there was a change in the school. Since Bernbaum's study there has been a vigorous debate at all levels over the nature and effects of the particular innovations involved. From being an expert-initiated 'non-political' innovation, the school became a focus for political controversy. This controversy led to an inspection of the school and a still continuing argument over the role of the local authority and its advisers *vis-à-vis* local schools.

Smith and Keith suggested in their Kensington study that the school paid too much attention to its national façade and too little to its local one. The very cosmopolitan nature of its teaching staff with their commitment to education rather than to this particular school reinforced this orientation and at Countesthorpe also there was a gradual awareness of this problem and attempts were made to come to terms with the school's local façade.

Throughout this work the view of innovators as neutral determiners of the education best suited to the population has been challenged. Arguing along similar lines Katz (1971, p. 136) has suggested educational innovation must be treated as a species of class activity reflecting an attempt at cultural imposition fully as much as traditional education with its emphasis on competition, restraint and orderliness. Attempts to clarify some of the problems in this area appear in Bernstein's later work (for a useful discussion of the background to this aspect of Bernstein's work see Davies, 1976, ch. 7). In his paper 'Class and pedagogies: visible and invisible' Bernstein (1975, ch. 6) suggests that changes in the complexity of the division of labour have led to the growth of a new middle class. He sees this new middle class as comprising those who are engaged in symbolic control, i.e. those who are filling the expanding major and minor professional class concerned with the servicing of people, e.g. medical and mental health specialists, social workers, media personnel and teachers. He claims that this group are concerned that their young be socialized as persons rather than individuals and that it is their ideology of education which is now firmly institutionalized in the infant school.

In Bernstein's analysis the conflict between the different educational ideologies is still seen as a clash between the ideologies of class, but as a clash between the ideologies of the old and the new middle class. However, he points out that the new middle class are caught in a contradiction, for their theories are at variance with their objective class position. If the new middle class is to repeat its position in the class structure, then appropriate secondary socialization into privileged education becomes crucial.

The essential dilemma is recognized in this extract from an interview with a self-employed engineer educated at Dartington Hall:

> I'd like my children to be able to live in the way that I am now and to have my values, moral values – if only I knew what they were! I wouldn't like them to lead unstable emotional lives, I'd like them to have good emotional relationships – that sounds pompous – they should have higher education, and it would be nice for one's ego if one was an engineer. I want them to be in a good competitive position in relation to the rest of the society but I wouldn't like them to be Freemasons or members of Lloyds. (Punch, 1977, p. 136)

Bernstein views the new middle class as having ambivalent enthusiasm for the invisible pedagogy for the early socialization of the child but settling for the visible pedagogy of the secondary school. In a final important section it is suggested that the new middle class can comfortably support the extension of the invisible pedagogy into the secondary school because the secondary school is likely to provide both visible and invisible pedagogies. The reproduction of class relationships in education is likely to remain unchanged because the visible pedagogies will be provided for the more able, i.e. those mainly drawn from middle-class backgrounds, while the invisible pedagogies will be provided for the less able, i.e. those more likely to be drawn from a working-class background.

Clearly Sharp and Green's work, already discussed in this chapter, begins to address itself to many of the problems Bernstein has raised. However, the analysis must be seen as largely exploratory. More work needs to be undertaken in terms of an analysis of the changing class system, not only leading to a clearer delineation of the features of the 'old' and the 'new' middle class but also looking more closely at changes within the working class. As well as exploration of the contemporary situation, careful analysis of previous periods of educational reform when similar educational ideologies were prevalent is needed. Bernstein's work does raise crucial, and much neglected, questions about the relationship of different groups in society to new pedagogies and stresses key questions of changes in power relationships between teachers and their clients, particularly working-class parents. As we have seen, however, these possible changes in the home–school power relationships are occurring at a time when many other features of the wider society, particularly the demographic changes, are likely to lend weight to the increasing demands for greater parental involvement in schools. Empirical research in this area should be an integral part of future studies in educational innovation.

# 7

# Students
# and innovation

Waller, in his classic work *The Sociology of Teaching,* claimed that,

> It is only because teachers wish to force students to learn, that any unpleasantness ever arises to mar their relationship . . . If this process were unforced, if students could be allowed to learn only what interested them, to learn in their own way, and to learn no more and no better than it pleased them to do, if good order were not considered a necessary condition of learning, if teachers did not have to be task-masters, but merely helpers and friends, then life would be sweet in the schoolrooms. These, however, are all conditions contrary to fact. (Waller, 1965, p. 365)

To Waller conflict arising out of the teacher–pupil relationship was a central fact in schools. Later studies have elaborated on this by showing how other features of schools, for example the organization of the school in terms of ability grouping, have accentuated the conflicts which Waller saw 'naturally' arising from the teacher–pupil relationship.

At the level of formal doctrine many of the large-scale innovations we have been looking at are attempting to challenge the view that such teacher–pupil conflict is endemic to schools. The theme running through them is that students should have greater autonomy in learning and that teachers should be non-authoritarian. While studies such as Hargreaves (1967) and Lacey (1970) suggest that schools organized along 'traditional' lines – subject-centred curriculum, didactic pedagogy, formal, authoritarian staff–student relationships and a differentiated system of ability grouping ('streaming') tend to produce polarized pro- and anti-school groups which reflect a considerable degree of conflict between staff and students, and among students themselves, what happens if a school is organized along quite different lines? Are we to accept the claims of the proponents of innovations such as 'open education' that informal staff–student relationships, a student-centred curriculum, an informal, heuristic pedagogy, an emphasis on personal, rather than positional authority, and the absence of any form of streaming will result in an unpolarized, conflict-free pattern of teacher–student and student–student relationships?

While little research has been carried out in this area, sociologists have been at pains to point out to innovators that they should not ignore the interaction between the organization of the school and the wider environment, particularly the system of social stratification which surrounds and penetrates it. As Willis (1976) has pointed out, studies of the sociology of the school and its students have centred on the cultural divisions in the school itself, and have tended to isolate the school from its surrounding network. The omission of the context in which the school operates has tended to imply that the institution be given primacy in the determination of the social landscape of the school. Willis's findings from his own study of the transition from school to work of white, working-class, average to low ability boys in a Midlands industrial conurbation support the view that there is a direct relationship between the main features of working-class culture, as it is expressed in shop-floor culture and school counter-culture. Both share broadly the same determinants: the common impulse is to develop strategies for dealing with boredom, blocked opportunities, alienation and lack of control.

Studies of innovative schools raise similar questions about the power of the school to transform the students' response to schooling and hence to prevent a school counter-culture developing. First it must be recognized that all innovative schools work within a framework of compulsory schooling. In this country, for example, all students are compelled by law to remain in school until sixteen and so for some students, however positive their reactions may be to any innovative school, it is likely to be the best of a bad job.

The dangers of ignoring the relationship between the school and its wider environment are well illustrated in Barth's study of an elementary school with a population two-thirds of whom were black, and where most of the families were on welfare. He claims that the children, from their prior experience, saw the school as a place where only two conditions could exist – firm authoritarian order or chaos. The children were merciless in their demands for teacher-imposed order and remained dependent upon adult control for any productive organized experience. The permissiveness of the teachers was frightening to children who knew only two alternatives in their previous experience with adults: neglect or firm control. The author even suggests that the permissiveness of the teachers might have looked to these children like a lack of concern – the very opposite of what the teachers wished to communicate.

The problems facing the innovative school are well illustrated in Sussman's (1974) American study of a high school. The administrators of the school claimed that the school was 'individualized' and that they were dealing with individuals not groups. They, therefore, denied the existence of student groupings within their school. Sussman showed that over 90 per cent of the students preferred this new system of individualized learning. However, later interviews made it clear that this large majority split into two main groups: those students who liked the innovation because it gave them more leisure time, and those who liked it because it taught them how to organize their time. The small minority of students who preferred the old system were explicit about their need for external controls if they were to do any work. These differing views of the innovations were closely related to the pattern of social interaction of the students. Although the high school had no streaming and schedules were individualized, the youngsters of lower socio-economic status streamed themselves into the shop, the industrial, the commercial and other vocational courses. Associated with these courses were student groupings which gave unflattering descriptions of each other. The college preparatory students referred to the place the vocational students spent their free time as the 'zoo' while the vocational students called the college preparatory students' meeting-place 'the country club'.

## Metro High School

The most detailed description in an innovative secondary school of the perceptions and behaviours of student sub-groups and their relationships to the wider environment is presented in the study of Metro High School in Chicago. Metro High School is an alternative high school without walls operating within the Chicago public school system (Center for New Schools, 1972). It was found that the groupings of students were still closely related to the life styles, attitudes towards schooling and patterns of association the students had developed in their previous schools and in the wider environment. The authors point to the existence of six main sub-groups within the school environment and attempt to place them in the context of the surrounding environment.

1 *Black School-Oriented*: The Black School-Oriented students conformed to the expectations of their previous schools, in terms of both academic performance and personal behaviour. They viewed school in terms of getting a good job and going to college. They tended to complete school work faithfully and had average to superior skill levels and records of past achievement. They came from lower to middle income background.

2 *Black-Consciousness/School-Oriented*: These students had many characteristics in common with the Black School-Oriented group. However, they were more aware of the political dimensions of the Black consciousness movement and talked about success in school as a means for gaining skills that would further Black political development.

3 *Black School-Alienated*: The previous experiences of these students had been characterized by academic failure and conflict with the school. They identified strongly with Black students from similar backgrounds. These students also identified with the aesthetic elements of Black consciousness in terms of dress and music. They tended to come from low-income families and often lived in large housing projects or physically decaying inner-city neighbourhoods.

4 *White School-Oriented*: These students had the same general characteristics as Black School-Oriented students.

5 *White School-Alienated/Ethnic*: These students had a history of past school experience similar to the Black School-Alienated students. Their family income levels fell in the low to middle range. Members of the group generally saw themselves as 'greasers', and thus acted out their alienation from the school in a manner that is consistent with the values of urban ethnic white youth. They were particularly hostile to the White School-Alienated/Youth Culture students.

6 *White School-Alienated/Youth Culture*: These students, mostly from middle-income backgrounds, identified with the 'Counter-culture'. They tended to be articulate and expressed radical political views. They may have recently failed in school because they were 'fed up with it', but their past school records included periods of high achievement, and they were generally above grade level in basic skills.

The existence of these sub-groups had dramatic effects on many of the innovative features of the Metro High School, particularly on student involvement in institutional decision-making. Almost every student who became involved in decision-making on a sustained basis came from the White School-Alienated/Youth Culture group. They shared the class background and life style of the majority of the faculty, were attuned to the same political issues as many faculty members and held the same ideas about the need for freedom in education and for the radical alteration of conventional schooling. In decision-making this resulted in the staff selecting issues for resolution that they deemed most important in terms of their own values. Thus the staff tended to serve the needs of students with value orientations and backgrounds similar to their own. For example, most of the staff shared the feeling of the White Youth Culture students that traditional school activities and symbols such as dances, class rings, school colours and cheer-leaders were unnecessary. The convergence of values among these two groups and their dominance of the decision-making apparatus obscured the strong interest among the School-Oriented and other School-Alienated groups in bringing some of these conventional school elements to Metro.

In this country administrators and teachers appear to have a growing awareness of the 'problems' arising from the differential reactions of students to innovation. Hannan (1975), in his study of an innovative Leicestershire upper school, shows how, particularly since the raising of the school-leaving age, much staff time in official and unofficial meetings has been concerned with the problem of the 'motivation of the unmotivated'. The continuing presence in the school of those who refused to accept or were in-capable of employing the learning styles laid down in the formal doctrine of the school aroused great concern. Bernbaum's study of Countesthorpe College in its early stages raised similar questions of how the staff would react to the differential motivation of the students. He noted that some students got on with their individual school work and accepted the guidance of the staff while others, lacking the skill and motivation necessary, did little and on occa-sions disrupted everyone. As one teacher put her recognition of the problem.

> Some children just can't discipline themselves to work . . . The drawback with our system is that the children who need to do the extra work are the ones who don't do it; the children who are interested and are good are the ones who go on and do more. (Bernbaum, 1973, p. 58)

More recent developments at Countesthorpe, such as the intro-duction of teams, seem to have been largely inspired by a continu-ing concern with this problem.

Despite recognition of the ways in which variations in the nature of the existing or potential student population are crucial in affecting new developments, such studies as have been con-ducted have relied on unsystematic observation. No research has been undertaken which has examined the reactions of pupils

102

to innovations in a more systematic manner involving the study of vital background variables such as social class, sex and age. Yet, clearly, research does show that the implementation of large-scale innovations involving change in the role of the teacher and the student requires a renegotiation of the contract between the teacher and the students. It is not the case that students are a clean slate passively waiting for teachers to inscribe their will on them (Nash, 1973). Students have clear expectations for the role of the teacher and the role of the students. Musgrove and Taylor's (1969) work on the expectations of pupils showed that pupils expected teachers to assume an essentially intellectual and instrumental role: all children gave most weight to the good teacher's teaching, least weight to his personal qualities. The crucial question is, are the students' expectations of teachers and schooling formed primarily by their experiences in schools or are they formed by their experiences outside the school situation and, therefore, not easily modifiable by changes in the school situation. There is some suggestion in Musgrove and Taylor's study that changes in the nature of the school organization can lead to changes in the expectations held by students. They note that children in un-streamed junior schools were significantly more concerned with the good teachers' personal qualities and those in streamed schools were more concerned with his discipline (Musgrove and Taylor, 1969, p. 24). Clearly more research is required in this field particularly in areas where students have spent the whole of their educational careers in 'progressive' schools.

Another area where little systematic research has been undertaken is that of the unintended consequences of such innovations for teacher–pupil and pupil–pupil relationships. It has been suggested that the withdrawal of the teachers' authority and the conventional structure of curriculum and regulations creates a vacuum which is filled by the authority of peer groups. Bernstein (1967), in an influential article entitled 'Open schools, open society', speculated on the implications of 'open schools' for adolescent peer groups. He suggested that in open schools staff and students were likely to experience a sense of loss of structure and with this problems of boundary, continuity, order and ambivalence were likely to arise. He claimed that a consequence of this would be a strengthening of the adherence of the pupils to their own age group as a major source of belief, relation and identity.

Other commentators have pointed to the importance of the study of students' orientations to the open school. Gibbons's vivid description of an open classroom in a New England high school points to a situation very similar to that suggested by Bernstein and highlights some of the unintended consequences for the student in the open school.

Life in our classroom was not necessarily more free or independent than life in the regular classrooms around us. Isolated in desks and controlled by regulations, students are protected from interference by others, from the threatening struggle for social status, from much of the pressure classmates might exert on their behaviour, and from the sustained visibility of individual performance. In our classroom . . . students worked constantly under the threat of interference; the first problem was to establish friendships, working relationships and status; there was sustained social pressure from classmates, intimidating and supportive; and each student was under constant observation by others, stripped of his usual classroom anonymity and privacy. It also seems evident that the controls of traditional curriculum and instruction do not necessarily deprive the student of independence. Textbooks, lessons and examinations all provide a structure within which the student can focus his individual efforts. In discussions, participation or indifference are both possible. In exercises and assignments he may work to take advantage of the protective minimum effort usually tolerated, or even conspire in the mild resistance of mischief – a convention of formal schooling. But in our class there were comparatively few structures to guide independent effort, and it was quite possible to languish in the limbo of confusion. Indifference was by definition failure. Resistance, awkward since many of the usual justifications of it were removed . . . Deficiencies usually hidden became glaringly evident to the student and others when he set out to read, compose, plan, discuss, lead and organize in the execution of an activity he chose himself and by the choice said, 'I will do the best I can'. (Gibbons in Sussman, 1974, p. 106)

Speculations about the nature of the relationship between open schooling and the adolescent society are not totally the province of the sociologist. It has already been suggested that some innovative educators, aware of the work of many social scientists, have incorporated such work into their reflection on their practice. In a recent publication on developments at Countesthorpe College, the second Warden admits that one consequence of the academic and social organization of the school has been an increase in the power of peer group conformity. This creates certain new problems for the teacher who now has to persuade a close-knit group of students rather than the differentiated, if larger group, of the orthodox classroom. He claims that the teacher '. . . will often find that having stepped out of his dominant role, one or another of his students will step into it and we must then face the question of whether the new dominance is less desirable all round than the old one. There is no easy solution, but in an authoritarian situation such a transfer of power from class teacher to peer group leader would be disastrous, leading inevitably to conflict. Within a participatory dispersal of power, however, where the Them–Us division is minimized, the situation is defused and becomes another basis for negotiation instead' (Watts, 1973b, p. 153).

In conclusion it is obvious that many questions still need to be answered about the nature of student relationships in the innovative school. What forms do student groupings take, what are their size and reasons for existence? How do they relate to the various staff groupings? Are they tightly knit, homogeneous closed groups with a high degree of group influence or loosely knit networks, heterogeneous in composition, relatively open and with a low degree of group consciousness? Do both co-exist? It is only by exploring issues such as these that the full significance of the changes in student relationships resultant upon any innovation can be realized and evaluated.

# 8

# Conclusion

The contemporary debate about the nature and significance of recent developments in progressive educational practice raises general questions about the role of research and its relationship to evaluation of innovation in education. Traditional models of evaluation which judge innovative school programmes on the basis of outcomes in limited areas of skill achievement measured over a short period of time have been challenged (see House, 1973 and 1974). Supporters of such models have often presented them as free from any concerns outside their science and have neglected to examine the consequences arising from the inescapably political nature of evaluation. At its simplest, evaluation is the process of applying a set of standards to a programme, making judgments using the standards, and justifying the standards and their application. In a society with differing value systems, the problem is whose standards are to apply in the evaluation process. If a proponent of an innovation wishes to defend it, he chooses the grounds on which it is evaluated; if a critic wishes to attack, he chooses different standards. As House points out, 'Whichever side the results favor will use them to gain political advantage. Evaluation becomes a tool in the process of who gets what in the society' (House, 1973, p. 3). A consequence of this is the argument that the primary latent function of many traditional evaluation studies is to provide a legitimization process for predetermined policies. Furthermore, it is not surprising to discover that evaluation results, both in education and in industry, are often only used when their findings are favourable (see Carter, 1973).

The progressive educator has viewed with suspicion this traditional model of evaluation. In more general terms, he has been wary of research and evaluation of progressive education believing that the cause would be better advanced by faith rather than by the accumulation of knowledge gained by empirical investigation (Ash, 1969). The world-view associated with progressive schooling stresses the value of sensitivity to individual people and situations and supports a view of each school as unique and having to struggle alone with its particular set of circumstances. It has been suggested (Center for New Schools, 1972) that there is one prevailing view to which many of the problems of progressive schools can be traced – the concept of 'organic growth'. The core assumption is that once people are freed from the oppressive restrictions of the traditional school, a new learning community will evolve naturally as people deal with each other openly and honestly. It is believed that it is easy for individuals to shed traditional values and attitudes and that 'from underneath the old skin will emerge a beautiful new man, new woman and new community' (Center for New Schools, 1972, p. 336).

Yet as we have seen in the last three chapters, schools influenced by this theory of organic development appear to generate remarkably similar sets of problems. Despite apparent early agreement, conflicts occur among staff holding different conceptions of the school's goals as well as conflicts between various groups of students. Staff begin to face problems in 'controlling' and 'motivating' students as patterns of differential response to school become apparent. There are problems in implementing direct democracy, in particular relating to the involvements of students in the decision-making process, and new decision-making structures have to be developed. Many writers sympathetic to the progressive school ethos are arguing that now is the time to abandon the traditional scepticism with which research and evaluation are viewed. If progressive schooling is to become an important influence, particularly in the state educational system, they argue it must learn from experience and attempt where possible to avoid the mistakes made by predecessors.

While there is some agreement on the necessity for a move away from traditional models and methods of research and evaluation, there is still controversy over the direction in which we should be moving. There is general consensus on the areas to be focused upon in this new research. It would concentrate upon a more intensive study of the day-to-day interactions in schools – interactions among students, between students and staff, among staff members and between the school and the outside world (see, for example, Center for New Schools, 1972). There is growing recognition of the need for multiple methods of research which would involve participant observation and informal interviewing as well as more structural techniques such as questionnaires and formal interviewing. Such research would, ideally, frequently take the form of a longitudinal study which would allow the investigation of important questions such as the development of sub-groups among the staff and student population, and the relationships between the school and the community. This would allow exploration of the extent to which the school was successful in achieving its broader aims such as how far had the school acted as an agent of change in the local and national community.

There is, however, less agreement on the question of the role the researcher is going to play. Some researchers, emphasizing the value-commitment that is implicit in all types of evaluation and research efforts in education, have suggested a new role as partisan. The researcher, it is argued, rather than being seen as a 'value-free' outsider, should be a committed but critical participant (Center for New Schools, 1972, p. 343). It is hoped that in this new role research and evaluation would play a crucial role in strengthening progressive schools. The researcher would see himself as contributing one of a number of perspectives on the school's growth, within a framework of shared analysis and decision-making, with the clear recognition that the researcher's claims to understand reality in a special way should be modest in the light of the primitive state of social science research. Attention has been particularly paid to one of the underdeveloped areas of traditional

108

research and evaluation – the question of information feedback.

Problems for the 'partisan' researcher are likely to arise because while ideally he wishes to confront the various audiences with his findings, in reality his relationships with one group, the staff, are likely to be strongest. These difficulties are recognized in the Center for New Schools study (1972, p. 349) where they note that their feedback approaches have been much less effective in reaching students than staff. The implications of 'commitment' have to be faced particularly in situations where there is fundamental disagreement. In conflict situations such as arose at the William Tyndale School it is important to explore what the role of the committed researcher would be. In a situation of conflict who would the researcher be committed to? Would, for example, groups who disagreed with the nature of the changes being made have an equally committed researcher and facilities available? This is most unlikely because, among other things, the promoters of innovation along with the staff of the school control access to it. The non-committed researcher may find it difficult to gain access to innovative schools; the staff believing that 'there is practically no place, or no rationale, for a disinterested role; one is either committed or one is simply not accepted' (Punch, 1977, p. 170). Researchers are likely to be viewed by the staff as either out to discredit progressive schools or to be careerists concerned with their own advancement in the academic community. Yet it is difficult to see how, without opening their doors both to the previously uncommitted as well as to the committed researcher, some of the important questions raised in this study can be answered.

# References and
# name index

# References and
# name index

*The numbers in italics after each entry refer to page numbers within this book.*

Argyris, G. (1971) *Management and Organizational Development.* New York: McGraw-Hill. *50*

Ash, M. (1969) *Who Are the Progressives Now?* London: Routledge and Kegan Paul. *107*

Auld, R. (1976) *The William Tyndale Junior and Infants School. Report of the Public Inquiry conducted by Mr. Robin Auld, Q.C. into the teaching, organization and management of the William Tyndale Junior and Infants School, Islington, London, N.1.* London: Inner London Education Authority. *86, 88–9*

Baldridge, J. V. (1971) *Power and Conflict in the University: Research in the Sociology of Complex Organizations.* New York: Wiley. *54–5*

Barker-Lunn, J. C. (1970) *Streaming in the Primary School: A Longitudinal Study of Children in Streamed and Non-streamed Junior Schools.* Slough: National Foundation for Educational Research. *25, 36*

Baron, G. and Tropp, A. (1961) Teachers in England and America. In A. H. Halsey, J. Floud and C. A. Anderson (eds) *Education, Economy and Society*. Glencoe, Ill.: Free Press. *84*

Barth, R. S. (1972) *Open Education and the American School*. New York: Agathon Press. *64, 70, 90, 99*

Becker, H. S. (1952) Social class variations in teacher–pupil relationship. *Journal of Educational Sociology*. *25, 29*

Bell, D. (1974) *The Coming of Post-Industrial Society: A Venture in Social Forecasting*. London: Heinemann. *17*

Bennett, S. N. and Jordan, J. (1975) A typology of teaching styles in primary schools. *British Journal of Educational Psychology 45* (1). *36–7*

Bennett, S. W. *et al.* (1976) *Teaching Styles and Pupil Progress*. London: Open Books. *36–7*

Bennis, W. G. (1966) *Changing Organizations: Essays on the Development and Evolution of Human Organization*. New York: McGraw-Hill. *49, 52*

Bennis, W. G. (1970) A funny thing happened on the way to the future. *American Psychologist 25*. *54*

Bennis, W. G., Benne, K. D. and Chin, R. (1969) *The Planning of Change* (2nd ed.) New York: Holt, Rinehart and Winston. *45*

Bereiter, C. (1973) *Must We Educate?* Englewood Cliffs, N.J.: Prentice-Hall. *82*

Berg, I. (1973) *Education and Jobs: The Great Training Robbery*. Harmondsworth: Penguin. *22–3*

Berg, L. (1968) *Risinghill: Death of a Comprehensive School*. Harmondsworth: Penguin. *60–1*

Berlak, A. C., Berlak, H., Bagenstos, N. T. and Mikel, E. R. (1975) Teaching and Learning in English primary schools. *School Review 83* (2). *39–40, 77*

Bernbaum, G. (1973) Countesthorpe College United Kingdom. In Centre for Educational Research and Innovation, *Case Studies of Educational Innovation: Vol. 3. At the School Level*. Paris: OECD. *77–8, 87, 94, 102*

Bernstein, B. (1967) Open schools, open society. *New Society*, 14 September. *103–4*

Bernstein, B. (1975) Class and pedagogies: visible and invisible. In *Class, Codes and Central*, Vol. 3. London: Routledge and Kegan Paul. *86, 94–6*

Berube, M. and Gittell, M. (eds) (1970) *Confrontation at Ocean Hill-Brownsville: The New York School Strikes of 1968*. New York: Praeger. *83*

Bowles, S. and Gintis, H. (1976) *Schooling in Capitalist America:*

*Educational Reform and the Contradictions of Economic Life.*
London: Routledge and Kegan Paul. *26–7*

Boyd, W. L. (1976) The public, the professionals and educational
policy making: who governs? *Teachers' College Record 77* (4). *83*

Boydell, D. (1971) *Survey of the Structure of Junior School Classrooms: Draft Report,* Leicester University School of Education.
*37, 77*

Bressler, M. (1963) The conventional wisdom of education and
sociology. In Page, C. H. (ed.) *Sociology and Contemporary Education.* New York: Random House. *53*

Brown, R. K. (1967) Research and consultancy in industrial enter-
prises: a review of the contribution of the Tavistock Institute of
Human Relations to the development of industrial sociology.
*Sociology 1. 55*

Brubaker, D. L. and Nelson, R. H. (1975) Pitfalls in the educational
change process. *Teachers College Record 26,* (1). *59*

Bruner, J. S. (1966) *Towards a Theory of Instruction.* Cambridge,
Mass.: Harvard University Press. *16*

Callaghan, J. (1976) Report of Ruskin College speech. *Education*
22 October. *25*

Cane, B. and Schroeder, C. (1970) *The Teacher and Research: A
Study of Teachers: Priorities and Opinions on Educational Research and Development:* Slough: NFER. *47*

Carlsson, R. O. (1964) Environmental constraints and organizational consequences: the public school and its clients. In D. E.
Griffiths (ed.) *Behavioural Science and Educational Administration.* Chicago: National Society for the Study of Education. *89*

Carter, R. K. (1973) Clients' resistance to negative findings. In
E. R. House *School Evaluation: The Politics and Process.* Berkeley: McCutchan. *107*

Center for New Schools (1972) Strengthening alternative High
Schools. *Harvard Educational Review 42.* (3). *100–2, 107–9*

Centre for Educational Research and Innovation (1973) *Case
Studies of Educational Innovation: Vol. 1. At the Central Level.
Vol. 2. At the Regional Level. Vol. 3. At the School Level. Vol. 4.
Strategies for Innovation in Education.* Paris: OECD. *61–2*

Charters, W. W. (1953) Social class analysis and the control of public education. *Harvard Educational Review 23. 81*

Chinoy, E. (1964) Popular sociology. In C. H. Page (ed.) *Sociology
and Contemporary Education.* New York: Random House. *38*

Clifford, G. J. (1973) A history of the impact of research on teaching. In R. M. V. Travers (ed.). *Second Handbook of Research on Teaching*. Chicago: Rand McNally. *32*

Coleman, J. S. *et. al.* (1966) *Equality of Educational Opportunity*. Washington: US. Department of Health, Education and Welfare. *23*

Collins, R. (1971) Functional and conflict theories of educational stratification. *American Sociological Review 36.* *23*

Collins, R. (1975) *Conflict Sociology*. New York: Academic Press. *23, 52, 57*

Corwin, R. G. (1973) *Reform and Organizational Survival: The Teacher Corps as an Instrument of Educational Change*. New York: Wiley. *49*

Cox, C. B. and Boyson, R. (eds) (1975) *Black Paper 1975: The Fight for Education*. London: Dent. *25*

Cremin, L. A. (1965) *The Wonderful World of Ellwood Patterson Cubberley: An Essay on the Historiography of American Education*. New York: Teachers College Press. *32*

Davies, B. (1976) *Social Control and Education*. London: Methuen. *94*

Delamont, S. (1976) *Interaction in the Classroom*. London: Methuen. *63*

Department of Education and Science (1966) *Report on Education 29: The Schools Council*. London: DES. *16*

Department of Education and Science (1972) *Education: a Framework for Expansion*. London: HMSO. *12*

Department of Education and Science (1977a) *Education in Schools. A Consultative Document*. London: HMSO. *82, 83*

Department of Education and Science (1977b) *A New Partnership For Our Schools*. Report of the Committee of Enquiry under the Chairmanship of Mr Tom Taylor. London: HMSO. *82*

Duane, M. (1968) The stench of hypocrisy. *Education*, 31 May. *85*

Eggleston, J. F., Galton, M. J. and Jones, M. (1976) *Processes and Products of Science Teaching*. London: Macmillan. *42*

Esland, G. (1972) *Innovation in the School*. Bletchley: Open University. *34*

Etzioni, A. (1966) *Studies in Social Change*. New York: Holt, Rinehart and Winston. *75*

Etzioni, A. (1971) Review of Charles E. Silberman's *Crisis in the Classroom*. *Harvard Educational Review 41* (1). *20*

116

Fisher, R. J. (1972) *Learning How to Learn: The English Primary School and American Education*. New York: Harcourt Brace. *84*

Floud, J. and Halsey, A. H. (1961) Introduction. In A. H. Halsey, J. Floud and C. A. Anderson (eds) *Education, Economy and Society: A Reader in the Sociology of Education*. Glencoe, Ill.: Free Press. *31*

Ford, J. (1969) *Social Class and the Comprehensive School*. London: Routledge and Kegan Paul. *25*

Gass, J. R. (1973) Preface to Centre for Educational Research and Innovation, *Case Studies of Educational Innovation: Vol. 1. At the Central Level*. Paris: OECD. *16*

Glaser, B. G. and Strauss, A. L. (1967) *The Discovery of Grounded Theory: Strategies of Qualitative Research*. Chicago: Aldine. *63*

Goodlad, J. I. *et al.* (1970) *Behind the Classroom Door*. Worthington, Ohio: Charles A. Jones. *41*

Goodlad, J. I. *et al.* (1974) *Looking Behind the Classroom Door*. Worthington, Ohio: Charles A. Jones. *14*

Gouldner, A. W. (1954) *Wildcat Strike*. Yellow Springs: The Antioch Press. *52*

Gross, N., Giacquinta, J. B. and Bernstein, M. (1970): Failure to implement a major organizational innovation. In M. W. Miles and W. W. Charters (eds) *Learning in Social Settings*. Boston: Allyn and Bacon. *66*

Gross, N., Giacquinta, J. B. and Bernstein, M. (1971) *Implementing Organizational Innovation: A Sociological Analysis of Planned Educational Change*. New York: Harper and Row. *63, 66–70, 76*

Grubb, W. W. and Lazerson, M. (1975) 'Rally' round the workplace: continuities and fallacies in career education. *Harvard Educational Review 45*, (4). *17*

Halsey, A. H. (1968) The public schools debacle. *New Society*, 25 July. *12*

Halsey, A. H., Floud, J. and Anderson, C. A. (eds) (1961) *Education, Economy and Society: A Reader in the Sociology of Education*. Glencoe, Ill.: Free Press. *12, 14, 16*

Hannan, A. (1975) The problem of the 'unmotivated' in an open school: a participant observation study. In S. Delamont and G. Chanan (eds) *Frontiers of Classroom Research*. Slough: NFER. *102*

Harbison, F. and Myers, C. A. (1964) *Education, Manpower and Economic Growth*. New York: McGraw-Hill. *13*

Hargreaves, A. (1977) *Progressivism and Pupil Autonomy*. Leeds University Department of Sociology, Occasional Papers No. 3. *26, 30*

Hargreaves, D. H. (1967) *Social Relations in a Secondary School*. London: Routledge and Kegan Paul. *30, 98*

Harris, A., Lawn, M. and Prescott, W. (1975) *Curriculum Innovation*. Milton Keynes: Open University. *24*

Henry, J. (1966) *Culture Against Man*. London: Tavistock. *64*

Hilsum, S. and Cane, B. (1971) *The Teacher's Day*. Slough: NFER. *47*

Hoffer, E. (1952) *The True Believer: Thoughts on the Nature of Mass Movements*. London: Secker and Warburg. *74*

House, E. R. (ed) (1973) *School Evaluation. The Politics and Process*. Berkeley: McCutchan. *106–7*

House, E. R. (1974) *The Politics of Educational Innovation*. Berkeley: McCutchan. *106*

Hoyle, E. (1970) Planned organizational change in education. *Research in Education 3*. *51*

Hoyle, E. (1972) *Problems: A Theoretical Overview*. Bletchley: Open University. *15–19*

Hoyle, E. (1975) Leadership and decision-making in education. In M. G. Hughes (ed.) *Administering Education: International Challenge*. London: Athlone. *52*


Illich, I. D. (1971) *Deschooling Society*. London: Calder and Boyars. *19*


Jackson, P. W. (1968) *Life in Classrooms*. New York: Holt, Rinehart and Winston. *63*

Jencks, C. *et al.* (1972) *Inequality: A Reassessment of the Effect of Family and Schooling in America*. London: Allen Lane. *23, 26*


Karier, C. J. (1973) Liberal ideology and the quest for orderly change. In C. J. Karier, P. C. Violas and J. Spring. *Roots of Crisis: American Education in the Twentieth Century*. Chicago: Rand McNally. *53*

Katz, M. B. (1971) *Class, Bureaucracy and Schools: The Illusion of Educational Change in America*. New York: Praeger. *94*

Klein, R. *et al.* (1974) *Social Policy and Public Expenditure 1974*. London: Centre for Studies in Social Policy. *11*

Kohn, M. L. (1969) *Class and Conformity: A Study of Values*. Homewood, Ill.: Dorsey. *91–2*

Lacey, C. (1970) *Hightown Grammar: The School as a Social System*. Manchester: Manchester University Press. *98*

Layard, R., King, J. and Moser, C. (1969) *The Impact of Robbins*. Harmondsworth: Penguin. *11*

Lewin, K. (1947) Group decision and social change. In T. Newcomb and E. Hartley (eds) *Readings in Social Psychology*. New York: Holt, Rinehart and Winston. *50*

Lewin, K. (1952) *Field Theory in Social Science: Selected Theoretical Papers*. London: Tavistock Publications. *45*

Lightall, F. F. (1973) Multiple realities and organizational non-solutions: an essay on anatomy of educational innovations. *School Review 81* (2). *62, 85*

Little, A. and Westergaard, J. (1964) The trend of class differentials in educational opportunity in England and Wales. *British Journal of Sociology 15* (4). *24*

Litwak, C. and Meyer, H. J. (1974) *School, Family and Neighbourhood: The Theory and Practice of School-Community Relations*. New York: Columbia University Press. *82*

Lortie, D. C. (1975) *School-Teacher: A Sociological Study*. Chicago: University of Chicago Press. *32*

Lynd, R. S. and H. M. (1929) *Middletown: A Study in American Culture*. New York: Harcourt, Brace. *80–1*

Lynd, R. S. and H. M. (1937) *Middletown in Transition: A Study in Cultural Conflicts*. New York: Harcourt, Brace. *80*

McMullen, T. (1968) Flexibility for a comprehensive school. *Forum 10* (2). *18*

McMullen, T. (1972) Countesthorpe College, Leicestershire. *Forum 14* (2). *85*

Makins, V. (1975) The story of Countesthorpe College and dividends of change. *Times Educational Supplement*, 16 and 23 June. *78*

Mann, D. H. (1976) *The Politics of Administrative Representation: School Administrators and Local Democracy*. Lexington: Heath. *83–4*

Marsden, D. (1972) Politicians, equality and comprehensives. In P. Townsend and N. Bosanquet (eds) *Labour and Inequality*. London. Fabian Society. *14*

Marshall, S. (1970) Threading pearls on the string of time. *Times Educational Supplement*, 27 February. *42–3*

Maslow, A. H. (1965) Observing and reporting education experiments. *Humanist 25* (13). *60*

Midwinter, E. (1973) The EPA Community School. *Urban Education 8.* 85

Miles, M. B. (1964) *Innovation in Education.* New York: Columbia University Press. *50*

Ministry of Education (1956) *Technical Education.* London: HMSO. *13*

Musgrove, F. and Taylor, P. H. (1969) *Society and the Teacher's Role.* London: Routledge and Kegan Paul. *84, 86, 88, 90, 103*

Myers, L. (1973) The opening of an open school. In D.A. and L. Myers (eds) *Open Education Re-examined.* Lexington: Heath. *64*

Nash, R. (1973) *Classrooms Observed: The Teacher's Perception and the Pupil's Performance.* London: Routledge and Kegan Paul. *103*

National Opinion Poll (1974) *Teachers in the British General Election of 1974.* London: Times Newspapers. *40*

Nisbet, J. (1975) Innovation – bandwagon or hearse? In A. Harris, M. Lawn and W. Prescott (eds) *Curriculum Innovation.* Milton Keynes: Open University. *24*

Plowden, Lady (1967) *Children and their Primary Schools: A Report of the Central Advisory Council for Education (England).* London: HMSO. *36–7, 84*

Psaltis, B. (1972) A humanistic experience: the British Primary Schools. In J. P. Cecco (ed.) *The Regeneration of the School: Readings in Educational Psychology, Sociology and Politics.* New York: Holt, Rinehart and Winston. *37–9*

Punch, M. (1977) *Progressive Retreat: A Sociological Study of Dartington Hall School and Some of its Former Pupils.* Cambridge: Cambridge University Press. *95, 109*

Reimer, E. (1971) *School is Dead.* Harmondsworth: Penguin. *19*

Remmling, G. W. (1974) *The Sociology of Karl Mannheim: Chaos or Planning?* London: Routledge and Kegan Paul. *19*

Richards, C. (1974) The Schools Council – a critical examination. *Universities Quarterly 28* (3). *47*

Richardson, E. (1973) *The Teacher, the School and the Task of Management.* London: Heinemann. *55–7*

Robbins, Lord (1963) *Committee on Higher Education.* London: HMSO. *13*

Robinson, D. W. (1972) An interview with Christopher Jencks. *Phi Delta Kappa 54.* *26*

120

Sarason, S. (1971) *The Culture of the School and the Problem of Change*. Boston: Allyn and Bacon. *48–9*

Schein, E. H. (1972) *Professional Education: Some New Directions*. New York: McGraw-Hill. *45, 50*

Schon, D. A. (1973) *Beyond the Stable State: Public and Private Learning in a Changing Society*. Harmondsworth: Penguin. *34*

Selleck, R. J. W. (1972) *English Primary Education and the Progressives 1914–39*. London: Routledge and Kegan Paul. *33–4*

Sharp, R. and Green, A. (1975) *Education and Social Control: A Study in Progressive Primary Education*. London: Routledge and Kegan Paul. *28–30, 86–8, 92–3, 95*

Shipman, M. D. with Bolam, D. and Jenkins, D. (1974) *Inside a Curriculum Project*. London: Methuen. *35–6*

Sieber, S. D. (1972) Images of the practitioner and strategies of educational change. *Sociology of Education 45*. *45–8*

Sieber, S. D. and Wilder, D. E. (1967) Teaching styles: parental preferences and professional role definitions. *Sociology of Education 40* (4). *90*

Silberman, C. E. (1970) *Crisis in the Classroom: The Remaking of American Education*. New York: Random House. *37–9*

Smith, L. M. and Keith, P. M. (1971) *Anatomy of Educational Innovation: Organizational Analysis of an Elementary School*. New York: John Wiley. *64, 70–7, 94*

Smith, W. O. Lester (1957) *Education: An Introductory Survey*. Harmondsworth: Penguin. *34*

Stephenson, T. E. (1975) Organization development – a critique. *Journal of Management Studies 12* (3). *52, 54, 57*

Sussman, L. (1974) The role of the teacher in selected innovative schools in the United States. In *The Teacher and Educational Change: A New Role*, Vol. 1. Paris: OECD. *99–100, 104*


Tannenbaum, R., Weschler, I. R. and Massarik, F. (1961) *Leadership and Organization*. New York: McGraw-Hill. *50–1*

Taylor, W. (1963) *The Secondary Modern School*. London: Faber. *42*

Taylor, W. (1975) The contribution of research to the study and practice of educational administration. In M. G. Hughes (ed.) *Administering Education: International Challenge*. London: Athlone. *47–8*

Tichy, N. M. (1974) Agents of planned social change: congruence of values, cognitions and actions. *Administrative Science Quarterly 19*. *51*

Tichy, N. M. (1975) How different types of change agents diagnose organizations. *Human Relations 28* (9). *45*

Vaizey, J. and Clarke, C. F. O. (1976) *Education: The State of The Debate in America, Britain and Canada.* London: Duckworth. *13–14*

Virtanen, L. (1973) Tapiola School, Finland. In Centre for Educational Research and Innovation, *Case Studies of Educational Innovation: Vol. 3. At the School Level.* Paris: OECD. *93–4*

Wallach, M. A. (1971) Essay review of the psychological impact of school experiences. *Harvard Educational Review 41* (2). *87*

Waller, W. (1965) (ed.) *The Sociology of Teaching.* New York: Wiley. *63, 97*

Watts, J. (1973a) Tell me what to do and I'll do it. In B. Turner (ed.) *Discipline in Schools.* London: Ward Lock. *18*

Watts, J. (1973b) Countesthorpe: A Case Study. In P. H. Taylor and J. Walton (eds) *The Curriculum: Research, Innovation and Change.* London: Ward Lock. *105*

Watts, J. (ed.) (1977) *The Countesthorpe Experience.* London: George Allen and Unwin. *18*

Westergaard, J. and Resler, H. (1975) *Class in a Capitalist Society: A Study of Contemporary Britain.* London: Heinemann. *24*

Willis, P. (1976) The class significance of school counter-culture. In M. Hammersley and P. Woods (eds) *The Process of Schooling: A Sociological Reader.* London: Routledge and Kegan Paul. *98*

Wilson, H. (1964) *The New Britain: Labour's Plan Selected Speeches 1964.* Harmondsworth: Penguin. *12*

Wylie, L. (1957) *Village in the Vaucluse.* Cambridge, Mass.: Harvard University Press. *33*

# Subject index

alternative of grandeur, 75–6
American elementary schools, 41–2, 62–78
  Cambire School, 63–4, 65–70, 75, 76, 92
  Kensington School, 64, 70–78, 85, 92, 94
Association for Science Education, 15
Autonomy
  educational system, 31
  school, 33
  teacher, 33, 41, 69, 81, 83, 84
  student, 98

Centre for Educational Research and Innovation, 16, 61–2, 93
Countesthorpe College, 17, 20, 77–9, 94, 102, 105
curriculum change, 15, 19, 20, 47

need for change in knowledge, 14, 15, 16
breakdown of barriers between subjects, 21, 33–4, 35

Dalton Plan, 33–4,
deschoolers, 18–19

economists, 11, 13, 22
education
  and jobs, 12, 22–3
  and poverty, 12, 26
  and social equality, 12, 13, 14, 23–4
  and the economy, 12–13, 22–3
  higher, 11, 23
  history of, 26–7, 32–4, 80
evaluation
  traditional models, 107
  and legitimation, 107
  and progressives, 107

facade, 73
formal doctrine, 72–3, 98
functionalism, 16, 30–1
    future society, images of, 16–20

H.M. Inspectors, 15, 36

Institutional Plan, 65–73, 77

Labour Party, 12–14, 88
L.E.A. Advisers, 35, 37

new middle class, 95–6
new intelligentsia, 17
Nuffield Foundation, 15, 20, 42

open classrooms/education, 27, 37, 39, 62–71, 98
organic development, 112
organizations,
    bureaucratic model, 51–2, 53–4
    human relations model, 52, 54
    political model, 53–5

Parents, 21, 53, 56, 60, 73, 79, 81
    and teachers in Britain, 83, 84, 86
    differing degrees of power, 86–9
    Parent-Teachers Association, 84
    perceptions of teachers, 86
    teachers' view of parents' life style, 28
    views of education, 89–92, 93
    working class parents' powerlessness, 86–7
population changes, 12, 22
public opinion polls, 14, 40, 41

Risinghill school, 60–1, 89

schema, 72–3
schools
    British primary, 20, 24–5, 28–30, 33–4, 36–41, 42–3
    Mapledene school, 28, 87, 92–3
    American observers, 37–40, 76, 87
    comprehensive, 14, 17–18, 25, 48, 60–1
    secondary, 14, 17, 42
Schools Council, 15, 42, 47, 82–3
science, 13, 15, 20, 42
    scientific and technical manpower, 13
social control, 30
social demand, 12
strategies of change, 45–51, 57
    empirical-rational, 46–8
    power-coercive, 46, 48–9
    normative re-educational, 46, 49–50, 55
status conflict theory, 23
streaming, 25, 36, 98
student
    assessment, 35
    change in learning procedures, 16, 20–1, 34, 35
    discipline, 35
    expectations of teachers, 102–3
    motivation, 35, 102, 107
    peer groups, 100–1, 103–5, 108
    views of innovations, 99, 102

teachers
    as rational man, 46–8
    attitudes to educational research, 47

autonomy, 41, 42, 61
child centred, 28
democracy, 78
head-principal relationships, 17, 48
pupil relationships, 17, 78–9, 97
science, 15, 41
teaching styles, change in, 16, 21, 34, 36–7, 66–7

technical function theory, 22–3
true believer, 73–4

William Tyndale school, 85, 88, 89, 109

views of innovation
conservative, 22, 25, 29–30
liberal, 26, 52–3
radical, 22, 25–7